OLYMPIAS; AND, THE TEMPLE OF GLORY

Borgo Press Books by VOLTAIRE

Candide: A Play in Five Acts
The Death of Caesar: A Play in Three Acts
Oedipus: A Play in Five Acts
Olympias and The Temple of Glory: Two Plays
Saul and David: A Play in Five Acts
Socrates: A Play in Three Acts
Two Voltairean Plays: The Triumvirate and Comedy at Ferney

OLYMPIAS; AND, THE TEMPLE OF GLORY

TWO PLAYS

VOLTAIRE

Translated and Adapted by Frank J. Morlock

THE BORGO PRESS
MMXIII

OLYMPIAS; AND, THE TEMPLE OF GLORY

Copyright © 2003, 2013 by Frank J. Morlock

FIRST EDITION

Published by Wildside Press LLC

www.wildsidebooks.com

DEDICATION

To Mike Lidsky, my friend of many years

CONTENTS

OLYMPIAS	9
CAST OF CHARACTERS	10
ACT I	11
ACT II	36
ACT III	60
ACT IV	88
ACT V	111
THE TEMPLE OF GLORY	133
CAST OF CHARACTERS	134
ACT I	139
ACT II	146
ACT III	159
ACT IV	170
ACT V	184
ACT II VARIANT	189
ABOUT THE TRANSLATOR	202

OLYMPIAS
A TRAGEDY IN FIVE ACTS

CAST OF CHARACTERS

CASSANDER, son of Antipater, King of Macedonia

ANTIGONUS, king of part of a region in Asia

STATIRA, Widow of King Alexander the Great

OLYMPIAS, daughter of Statira and Alexander the Great

HIGH PRIEST, who presides over the celebration of great mysteries

SOSTERNES, officer of Cassander

HERMAS, officer of Antigonus

PRIESTS

GUESTS

PRIESTESSES

SOLDIERS and POPULACE

ACT I

The action takes place in the Temple of Ephesus, where the great mysteries are being celebrated. The stage represents the temple, the peristyle and the square leading to the temple.

The back of the stage represents a temple whose three closed doors are decorated with large pilasters; the two wings form a vast peristyle. Sosternes is in the peristyle, the large door opens. Cassander, worried and agitated, comes to him; the large door closes.

CASSANDER:

Sosternes, they are going to finish these terrible mysteries.

Cassander hopes at last the gods will be less inflexible.

My life will be more pure, and my feelings less troubled;

I breathe.

SOSTERNES:

Lord, near Ephesus are assembled

The warriors who served under the king, your father.

From my hands they've taken the customary oath.

Already your laws are recognized in Macedonia.

Ephesus has chosen between its two protectors.

This honor that Antigonus shares with you

Is an august omen of your great plans.

This reign which begins in the shadow of these altars

Will be blessed by the gods, and cherished by mortals.

This name of initiate, that is revered and loved,

Adds a new luster to the supreme grandeur.

Appear.

CASSANDER:

I cannot: your eyes will be the witnesses

Of my first devotions and my first efforts.

Stay in this sanctuary. Our august priestesses

Are presenting Olympias to erected altars.

She is expiating in secret, placed between their arms,

My unfortunate crimes that she is unaware of.

From today, I am beginning a new life.

Dear and tender Olympias, may you be forever

In ignorance of this great, painfully effaced crime

And of the blood of your birth and the blood I shed.

SOSTERNES:

What! lord, a child taken from the Euphrates

By your father already dedicated to service

On whom you extend so many generous cares

Could hurl Cassander into these terrible troubles!

CASSANDER:

Respect this slave to whom all owe homage:

I am repairing the outrage of fate that degrades her.

My father had his reasons for hiding her rank from her.

That must give to her the splendor of her blood—

What am I saying? O memory! O times! O day of crimes!

Sosternes, he counted her in the number of his victims.

He would have sacrificed her to our safety—

Nourished in carnage and cruelty.

Alone, I took pity on her, and I softened my father.

Alone, I knew the daughter having struck the mother.

She's still unaware of my crime and my furor.

Forever keep your error, Olympias!

In Cassander you cherish a benefactor and a master.

If you knew who you were you would detest me.

SOSTERNES:

I will penetrate no further these astonishing secrets,

And I am coming to you only to speak of your interests.

Lord, of all these kings that we see pretend

With so much furor to the throne of Alexander,

Your only ally is the inflexible Antigonus.

CASSANDER:

I've always respected friendship with him,

I will be faithful to him.

SOSTERNES:

He must also do so to you;

But since we've seen him appear within these walls,

It seems that in secret a jealous emotion

Has altered his heart and distances him from you.

CASSANDER:

(aside)

And who cares about Antigonus! O manes of Alexander!

Manes of Statira! Great shade! August ashes!

Remains of a demi-god, justly incensed,

Does my remorse and my passion avenge you enough?

Olympias, obtain from their appeased shade

That peace so long refused to my heart.

And let your virtue, dissipating my terror,

Be my protection here, and speak to the gods for me.

Eh, what! Towards this sanctuary, just hardly opened

Antigonus is approaching, and preceding the dawn!

(Enter Antigonus and Hermas.)

ANTIGONUS:

(to Hermas at the back of the stage)

This secret pesters me, it must be torn out.

I will read in his heart what he thinks to hide from me.

Go, don't go too far away.

CASSANDER:

(to Antigonus) When day's hardly lit,

What subject is so pressing that it brings you to me?

ANTIGONUS:

Our interests, Cassander. After your expiations

Hereabouts have satisfied the gods,

It is time to think of sharing the earth.

From Ephesus in these grand days they spare war.

Your secret mysteries, respected by nations,

Suspend discord and calamities.

It's a time of rest for the furors of princes

But this repose is short, and soon our provinces

Return to the prey of flames and battles

That the gods stop and that they don't extinguish.

Antipater is no more; your efforts, your courage,

No doubt, will finish his important work.

He would never have permitted that ingrate Seleucus,

The insolent Lagidus, the traitorous Antiochus,

Devouring the conquests of entombed Alexander,

Dare to brave us and march on our heads.

CASSANDER:

Would to the gods that Alexander on these ambitious

Were from the height of his throne to lower his eyes.

Would to the gods that he lived!

ANTIGONUS:

I cannot comprehend you.

Is it for the son of Antipater to weep for Alexander?

What can inspire you with such an urgent remorse?

After all, you are innocent of his death.

CASSANDER:

Ah! I caused his death.

ANTIGONUS:

It was legitimate.

All the Greeks were demanding this great victim.

The universe was weary of his ambition.

Athena, Athena even sent the poison.

Perdiccas received it; they charged Craterus with it.

It was placed in your hands, by the hands of your father.

Without his confiding in you this important plan

You were still young; you served at the festival,

At this last feast of the tyrant of Asia.

CASSANDER:

No, stop excusing this impious sacrilege.

ANTIGONUS:

This sacrilege! Eh, what! Your downtrodden spirit's

Setting up as a god the assassin of Cleitus,

The bloody executioner of the great Parmenio,

This proud fool who, stigmatizing his mother,

Really dared to aspire to the rank of the son of gods

And dishonored his mother to make himself adored?

He alone acted a sacrilege, and when at Babylon

We had overturned his altars and his throne,

When the fatal blow had ended his fate,

They avenged the gods and the human race.

CASSANDER:

I confess his faults, but whatever he may have been,

He was a great man and he was our master.

ANTIGONUS:

A great man!

CASSANDER:

Yes, without doubt.

ANTIGONUS:

Ah! It's our valor,

Our arms, our blood, which founded his grandeur;

He was just an ingrate.

CASSANDER:

O my tutelary gods!

What mortals were more ungrateful than our fathers?

All wanted to climb to this superb rank.

But why pierce the flank of his wife?

His wife! His children! Ah! What a day, Antigonus!

ANTIGONUS:

After fifteen years, this scruple astonishes me.

Jealous of his friends, the son-in-law of Darius,

He was becoming Persian; we were the vanquished.

Would you really want that, the proud Statira

Avenging Alexander's ashes in Babylon

Raising his subjects had sacrificed all of us

To the blood of her family, to the blood of her spouse?

She armed the whole populace; Antipater escaped

The furors of the queen with difficulty that day.

You were spared a father.

CASSANDER:

It is true, but still,

The wife of Alexander perished by my hand.

ANTIGONUS:

That's the fate of battles; the success of our arms

Ought not to cost us regrets and tears.

CASSANDER:

I admit it, I poured that frightful cup,

And covered with this august and unfortunate blood,

Astonished by myself and confused with rage

Through which my father dragged my blind courage,

I have for a long while lamented.

ANTIGONUS:

But, what secret motives

Increase today such keen regrets?

I have some right to read the heart of a friend.

You dissimulate too much.

CASSANDER:

Friend—what can I say?

Believe that there's a time in which the embattled heart fought

Though a secret instinct flies back towards virtue,

And from our criminal attempts, the past memory

Returns with horror to terrify thought.

ANTIGONUS:

Trust me, forget these expiated murders,

But let our interests not be forgotten.

If some repentance still bothers your life,

Repent especially for abandoning Asia

To the insolent law of traitorous Antiochus.

Let my brave warriors and your unvanquished Greeks

Make the Euphrates tremble a second time

Of all the new kings whose grandeur dazzles.

None is worthy of being one, nor in his early years

Served like us, under the conqueror of the Persians.

All our chiefs have perished.

CASSANDER:

I know it and perhaps

God sacrificed them to the Manes of their master.

ANTIGONUS:

We remain, we are living and we must rebuild

This debris, all embloodied, that we must collect.

Dying, Alexander left it to the most worthy.

I dare to seize it; his order designates me.

Assure my fortune thus, like your fate.

The most worthy of all, no question, is the strongest.

Let's raise again with our Greeks, the power destroyed,

Never let discord be introduced amongst us.

Nor expose ourselves anew to these new tyrants

They, who were not born to march as our equals.

Do you promise me?

CASSANDER:

Friend, I swear to you

I am ready to avenge our common insult.

The scepter of Asia is in unworthy hands

And the Euphrates and the Nile have too many sovereigns.

I will fight for myself, for you, and for Greece.

ANTIGONUS:

I believe your interest in it, I trust your promise about it.

And especially, I pride myself on the noble friendship

Whose respectable bonds have linked you to me.

But of this friendship I demand a pledge.

Don't refuse me.

CASSANDER:

That doubt is an outrage.

Is what you are asking in my power?

It's an order for me, you have only to wish it.

ANTIGONUS:

Perhaps you will see with some surprise

The little that friendship authorizes me to demand.

I only wish a slave.

CASSANDER:

Happy to serve you,

They are all at your feet, it's up to you to choose.

ANTIGONUS:

Allow me to demand a young foreigner. (looking at Cassander attentively)

One who your father carried off from the walls of Babylon.

She is your share: award me this prize

For so many happy labors undertaken on your behalf.

They say your father persecuted her.

I shall take care that at my court she will be respected.

Her name is Olympias.

CASSANDER:

Olympias!

ANTIGONUS:

Yes, lord.

CASSANDER:

(aside)

With what unexpected darts he comes to pierce my heart!

How can I give up Olympias!

ANTIGONUS:

Listen, I flatter myself

That Cassander doesn't have an ungrateful soul towards me.

A refusal of the least objects can be wounding

And doubtless you do not wish to offend me?

CASSANDER:

No; you will soon see this young captive.

You yourself shall judge if it is necessary that she follow you,

If it can be permitted to me to put her in your hands.

This temple is forbidden to profane humans;

Under the vigilant eyes of gods and goddesses,

Olympias is guarded in the midst of priestesses.

The doors will open when it is time.

In this sanctuary open to the rest of mortals,

New mysteries could surprise you there

And you will decide if the earth has kings

Who can enslave Olympias to their laws.

(Cassander goes back into the temple and Sosternes leaves.)

HERMAS:

(coming forward) Lord, you astonish me; when Asia in alarms

Sees a hundred bloody thrones battled over by armies,

When from the vast realms of entombed Alexander

Fortune is preparing a new division

When you pretend to a sovereign empire

A slave is the object to which your great heart aspires!

ANTIGONUS:

You ought to be astonished by it. I have reasons, Hermas,

That I dare not tell, and that no one knows.

Perhaps the fate of this slave is important

To all the kings of Asia; to whoever wants to be,

To whoever in his breast bears a heart grand enough

To dare to be the successor of Alexander.

On the name of slave and her adventures

I've long formed strange conjectures.

I wanted to enlighten myself; from these ramparts my eyes

Have sometimes rested their glance on her.

Her features, these parts, the time wherein heaven made her born,

The astonishing respect she receives from a master,

Cassander's remorse, and his dark speech

Have loaned aid to these secret suspicions.

I believe I've penetrated this shadowy mystery.

HERMAS:

They say that he cherishes her

And that he raises her like a father.

HERMAS:

We shall see—But it's opening up and this sacred temple

Is revealing to us an altar decorated with garlands.

I see priestesses appearing from both sides;

In the depth of the sanctuary the high priest is seated.

Olympias and Cassander have reached the altar.

(The three doors of the Temple have opened. The whole interior is revealed. Priests are on one side, Priestesses on the other. They are all dressed in white robes with blue belts whose ends descend to the ground. Cassander and Olympias place their hands on the altar. Antigonus and Hermas remain in the peristyle with a group of the People who appear at the sides.)

CASSANDER:

God of kings and of gods, eternal, unique being,

God revealed to me in these august ceremonies

Who punishes the perverse, who sustains the just,

Near whom remorse effaces crime,

Confirm, Clement God, the oath I have taken!

Receive these oaths, adorable Olympias:

I submit to your sway, my throne and my life.

I swear to you a love as pure, as holy

As that of the fire of Vesta which is never extinguished.

And you, daughters of heaven, you august priestesses,

Bear with the incense, my vows and my promises

To the thrones of the gods who deign to hear me

And ward off the darts that I may deserve.

OLYMPIAS:

O gods in whom I hope, forever protect

The generous master who treated me as a father,

My adored lover, my respectable spouse,

Let him be forever cherished, always worthy of you!

My heart is known to you. His rank and his crown

Are the least of the treasures that his love is giving to me.

Witness the tender flames inspired in my heart,

Be the guarantee of them, you who consecrate them.

Let him teach me to please you and that your justice

Prepare me for the hell of an eternal death,

If, unfaithful to your laws I for a moment forget

Both the condition in which I am and what I owe to him.

CASSANDER:

Let's go back into the sanctuary

Where my happiness is calling me.

Priestesses, dispose the solemn pomps

By which my happy life is going to commence its course.

Sanctify my life, and our chaste love.

I've seen the gods in temple, and I've seen them in her.

If I am faithless, let me be hated by all!

Antigonus, in these parts you heard me;

To the wishes you were expressing have I responded enough?

You yourself pronounce if you ought to pretend

To see the slave of Cassander in your hands.

Know that my crown and all my grandeur

Are weak presents, unworthy of her heart.

Let strict friendship unite the two of us;

Judge, if I ought to make such a sacrifice.

(He reenters the temple; the doors shut; the populace leaves the sanctuary.)

ANTIGONUS:

Go, I no longer doubt it and everything is revealed to me.

He intends to brave me; but be certain he will ruin himself.

I recognize in him impetuous rashness

Which sometimes serves the gods, and sometimes offends them.

This ardent character which joins passion

To politics and religion;

Swift, clever, proud, impetuous and tender,

Ready to repent, ready to do anything.

He marries a slave! Ah! You can really believe

That love knew how to abase him to this degree.

This slave is of a rank that he himself respects.

The plot of his hidden plans is very suspect.

He secretly flatters himself that Olympias has rights

Which can raise him to the rank of king of kings.

If he were only a lover he would have made me a confidant

Of a passion that was carrying him away with such violence.

Go, you will soon see implacable hate

Succeed without pity his weak friendship.

HERMAS:

To his distracted heart, perhaps you impute

Deeper plans than love has given birth to.

In our great interests, often our actions

Are, you know quite well, the result of passions.

Idly, one disguises their tyrannic power.

The weak sometimes pass for politic

And Cassander is not the first sovereign

Who cherished a slave and gave her his hand.

I have seen more than one hero subdued by his flame.

Overbearingly proud with kings, weak with a woman.

ANTIGONUS:

You say only too true; I am weighing your reasons,

But all that I've seen confirms my suspicions.

Shall I tell you them in the end? The charms of Olympias

Perhaps bring jealousy into my heart.

You pierce only too well my secret feelings.

Love is joining itself to these great interests

Their marriage wounds me more than I thought.

Is Cassander alone the prey of weakness?

HERMAS:

But he's counting on you. The most holy titles

Could they ever unite sovereigns?

The alliance, the gifts, the brotherhood of arms,

Your shared perils, your common alarms,

Your redoubled oaths, so many efforts, so many vows,

Don't they serve for anything

Except misfortune for the two of you?

Of sacred friendship isn't he most exemplary?

ANTIGONUS:

Friendship, I know, has temples in Greece.

Interest does not, but it is adored.

No question, from ambition and intoxicated love,

Cassander has deceived me about Olympias' fate.

Cassander hides from my enlightened eyes.

He's only too right to do so. Go, perhaps today

The object of so many wishes is not yet his.

HERMAS:

He received her hand— This sacred precinct

Sees the pomp of marriage already prepared.

(The initiates, the priests, and the priestesses cross the back of the stage, with palms decorated with flowers in their hands.)

HERMAS:

All the initiates, followed by their priests

Palms in hand are flooding this sanctuary.

And the most tender love is ordering this feast.

ANTIGONUS:

No, I tell you, his conquest can still be ravished from him.

Come, I will confide everything to your zeal, to your fidelity.

I will have laws, gods, the populace, for me.

For now, let's flee these pomps that outrage me.

Let's enter into the course where my plans are leading me.

If possible, let's water these holy asylums

Less with the blood of bulls, than the blood of humans.

CURTAIN

ACT II

This scene is intended to take place in the interior of the temple, but as most theaters are rarely constructed in a manner favorable to acoustics, the actors are obliged to come forward into the peristyle; but the three open doors show that you are in a temple.

HIGH PRIEST:

What! during these sacred days! What! In this august temple,

Where God pardons crime and consoles the just,

A single priestess would dare to deprive us

Of expiations that she must complete?

What! Arzana dispenses with such a holy duty?

A PRIESTESS:

Arzana is in retreat, obstinate and silent,

Irrigating the images of the gods with her tears.

Lord, you know it, hiding herself from all eyes,

In prey to her troubles, weakened by languor,

She implores an end to a dying life.

HIGH PRIEST:

We pity her condition; but she must obey.

She can serve for a short while at the altars.

Since she was confined to this temple

Today is the only day that fate has designated to her.

Let her be made to come. (The Priestess goes to seek Arzana)

The will of heaven

Demands her presence and calls her to the altar.

Olympias, crowned by her with garlands of flowers

Will be led in triumph to the gods.

Cassander, initiated in our divine secrets,

Will be purified by her august hands.

All must be accomplished. Our rites, our mysteries,

These directions that the gods have given to our fathers,

Cannot be changed, are not to any degree uncertain,

Like feeble laws invented by humans. (Statira, escorted by the Priestess, returns) (to Statira) Come, you cannot contradict yourself

By refusing to fulfill your holy ministry.

From the moment you pronounced irrevocable vows

In this sacred asylum,

This great day is the only one that God has chosen for you

To announce his decrees to the conquerors of Asia.

Be worthy of God whom you represent.

STATIRA:

(covered with a veil which hangs over her face without hiding it, and dressed like other priestess)

O heaven! For the last fifteen years within these secluded walls,

In the shadow of silence, inaccessible to the world,

I have enshrouded my horrible destiny.

Why are you drawing me from my obscurity?

You want to surrender me today, to calamity.

(to High Priest) Ah! lord, when I came to these abodes

It was to weep, to die unknown.

You know it.

HIGH PRIEST:

Heaven has prescribed other laws for you

And when you preside for the first time

At the pomps of marriage, at our grand mystery,

Your name, your rank, can no longer be hidden;

It must be spoken.

STATIRA:

Lord, what does it matter who I am?

The most abject blood, the blood of the greatest kings,

Aren't they equal before the Supreme Being?

It is indeed known to him more than his own.

In the past these great names were able to flatter me.

In the night of the tomb they must be carried off.

Leave me forever lost to memory.

HIGH PRIEST:

No question we renounce pride and glory.

We think as you do; but the Divinity

Exacts a simple admission, and wants the truth.

Speak— You are shaking.

STATIRA:

You yourself will shake.

(to priests and priestesses) You who serve with God the supreme majesty,

Who share my fate, attached to his cult,

May my secrets be hidden between you and this God.

HIGH PRIEST:

We all swear it to you.

STATIRA:

Before having heard me

Tell me if it is true that the cruel Cassander

Will be here in the rank of our initiates.

HIGH PRIEST:

Yes, madam.

STATIRA:

He's seen his crimes expiated!

HIGH PRIEST:

Alas! All humans have need of clemency.

If God didn't open his arms except to the sole innocent,

Who would come into this temple to burn incense on the altars?

God makes repentance the virtue of mortals.

This paternal judge sees from the height of his throne

The very culpable earth and his kindness pardons.

STATIRA:

Well, if you knew for what excess of horror

He demands mercy and fears a vengeful god,

If you were instructed that he made his master perish,

And what a master, great gods! if you could know

What blood he shed in our enflamed walls,

When before the barely closed eyes of Alexander,

Having dared to pierce his lamenting widow,

He threw her dying on the body of her spouse.

You will be more surprised when you learn

Of secrets that until now the earth was unaware of.

This wife raised to the fulfillment of glory

Whose Persian blood honored the memory,

Widow of a demi-god, daughter of Darius.

She is speaking to you here, don't question her any further.

(The priests and the priestesses raise their hands and bow.)

HIGH PRIEST:

O gods! What have I heard? Gods how the crime outrages.

With what blows you strike those who are your image!

Statira in this temple! Ah! Permit that at your knees

My deep respect—

STATIRA:

High Priest, raise yourself

I am no longer for you the mistress of the world.

Only respect here my profound sorrow.

See the fate of grandeurs down here.

What my father endured at the moment of his death,

In Babylon, in blood, I endured the same.

Darius, King of Kings, deprived of his diadem,

Fleeing in the deserts, wandering, abandoned,

Saw himself assassinated by his own friends.

A stranger, a pauper, a reject of the earth,

Comforted the misery of his last moments. (pointing to the Priestess who brought her)

Do you see this foreign woman in my court?

Her hand, her hand alone saved my life.

She alone drew me from the bloody crowd

Where my cowardly friends left me expiring.

She is an Ephesian, she guided my steps

Into this august asylum, at the end of my realm.

I saw myself despoiled by a thousand hands,

The country strewn with dead and dying.

Alexander's soldiers all raised up as kings

And public larcenies called great exploits.

I held in horror the world, and the ills it begets

Forever distant from it I will inter myself alive.

I confess, I weep for an infant daughter

Torn from my arms, from my embloodied body.

This foreign girl clings to me like family.

I lost Darius, Alexander, and my daughter.

God alone remains to me.

HIGH PRIEST:

Alas! May he be your support!

From the throne on which you were placed you rose almost to him.

His temple is your court; may it be happier here

Than in that august and dangerous grandeur,

On that terrible throne and by you forgotten

Become for the earth an object of pity.

STATIRA:

Lord, this temple has sometimes consoled me,

But you must feel the horror which troubles me

In seeing Cassander speak there to the same gods

That my prayers have implored against his impious head.

HIGH PRIEST:

The sacrifice is great: I feel deeply what it costs.

But our law speaks to you and your heart is listening;

You have embraced it.

STATIRA:

Would I had been able to foresee

That it would impose on me this horrible duty?

I feel that my life, worn out in bitterness,

Its torch paling to extinction and self-consumption,

In these last moments that God wishes to give me,

To what are they going to serve?

HIGH PRIEST:

Perhaps to forgive.

You yourself have depicted your career.

March in it without ever turning back.

The Manes, freed from a body, vile and mortal

Experience an eternal repose without passions.

A new day lights them: this day is without clouds.

They live for the gods: such is our portion.

A happy retreat leads to the depth of hearts,

Forgetfulness of enemies and forgetfulness of misfortunes.

STATIRA:

It's true, I was queen and am only a priestess.

In my horrid duty support my weakness.

What is it I must do?

HIGH PRIEST:

Olympias on her knees

Must first of all throw herself before you in these parts.

It's up to you to bless this illustrious marriage.

STATIRA:

I am going to prepare her for a life of misfortune.

It's the fate of mankind.

HIGH PRIEST:

The sacred fire, the incense,

The lustral water, the gifts offered to powerful gods,

All will be presented by your respectable hands.

STATIRA:

And for whom, wretch! Ah! My deplorable life,

Unto its last moment will it be charged with horror?

In this retreat I thought to avoid my misfortune

Misfortune is everywhere, I was abusing myself.

Come, let's follow the law imposed by myself

HIGH PRIEST:

Goodbye. I admire you more than I pity you.

She's coming to you. (he leaves)

(The stage shakes.)

STATIRA:

You are shaking,

Funereal and holy place! I hear a horrible murmur,

The temple is tottering! What! All nature

Is moved by its aspect! And my forlorn senses

Are in the same difficulty, and remain confounded!

OLYMPIAS:

(terrified) Ah! Madame!

STATIRA:

Approach, young and tender victim.

This frightening augury seems to announce crime;

Your attractions seem born only for virtue.

OLYMPIAS:

Just gods, support my downtrodden courage!

And you, confidant of their august decrees,

Deign to direct my innocent youth.

I am in your hands; dissipate my terror.

STATIRA:

Ah! I've got more of it than you! My child, hug me.

Are you informed of the fate of your spouse?

What is your country? What blood has conceived you?

OLYMPIAS:

Humble in my condition, I haven't expected

This rank to which they are raising me, and which is not owed me.

Cassander is king, madame; in Greece in his father's court,

He deigned to raise my youth.

Since I fell into his august hands

I've always seen in him the greatest of humans.

I cherish a spouse and I revere a master.

Behold all my feelings, and behold all my being.

STATIRA:

Just heaven, how easily a young heart is deceived!

I love the candor of innocence in you!

So, Cassander has taken care of your destiny?

What! You were not born of a prince or a king?

OLYMPIAS:

To love virtue and follow its laws,

Must one be born in the purple of kings?

STATIRA:

No, I see only too much crime on the throne.

OLYMPIAS:

I was only a slave.

STATIRA:

Such a destiny astonishes me.

The gods have placed nobility

On your face, in your eyes, in your features,

As well as attractions.

You, slave!

OLYMPIAS:

Antipater, in my first infancy

By the fate of combat held me under his power.

I owe everything to his son.

STATIRA:

Since your earliest days

Experienced misfortune and saw the end of its course!

And mine has lasted the whole time of my life!

In what times and in what parts were you pursued

By this frightful destiny which put you in irons?

OLYMPIAS:

They say that they ended the life

Of a great king, master of the universe,

They were splitting up his empire and that in Babylon

Cassander saved my unfortunate life

Abandoned to the sword during the horror and carnage.

STATIRA:

What! In the times marked by the death of Alexander

Captive of Antipater, and obedient to Cassander?

OLYMPIAS:

That's all that I've learned. So many misfortunes passed

Are to be effaced by my new happiness.

STATIRA:

Captured in Babylon! O eternal power!

Are you making a sport of the tears of a mortal woman?

The place, the time, her age, have excited in me

Joy and sorrow, tenderness and terror.

Am I not deceiving myself? Heaven seems to imprint on her face

The image of my heroic spouse.

OLYMPIAS:

What are you saying?

STATIRA:

Alas! Such were his looks,

When, less proud and more soft, far from bloody dangers,

Raising my family robbed by the sword,

He restored it to the rank from which it had fallen.

When his hand joined to my trembling hand.

Illusion too dear, faltering and idle hope!

Is it possible? Listen to me, princess;

Have some pity on the trouble that presses me.

Do you have any recollection of a mother?

OLYMPIAS:

Those who from my infancy were able to talk to me

Told me all about that time of trouble and carnage.

From leaving the cradle I was enslaved.

I've never known a mother's love.

I am unaware who I am, and who gave me life.

Alas! You are sighing, you are weeping, and my tears

Are mixed with your tears, and I find charms in that—

Eh, what! You clasp me in your languishing arms!

You are making impotent efforts to speak!

Speak to me.

STATIRA:

I cannot—I am succumbing—Olympias!

The trouble I am feeling is going to cost me my life.

(Enter the High Priest.)

HIGH PRIEST:

O priestess of gods! O queen of humans!

What new change in your sad destiny!

What must we do, and what are you going to hear?

STATIRA:

Misfortunes; I am prepared and I must expect all.

HIGH PRIEST:

It's the greatest of blessings mixed with bitterness

But there's no alternative. Antigonus troubled,

Antigonus, his partisans, the populace, the armies

Animated by zeal, all at last voice,

All say that this creature present to your eyes,

Who for a long while was in obscurity like you,

That your royal hands are going to unite with Cassander,

That Olympias—

STATIRA:

Get it over with.

HIGH PRIEST:

Is Alexander's daughter.

STATIRA:

(running to embrace Olympias)

Ah! My lacerated heart told me that before you did.

O my daughter! O my blood! O sweet and fatal name.

In your embrace, I must rejoice,

Though by your marriage you are causing my death!

OLYMPIAS:

What! You are my mother and you lament over it!

STATIRA:

No, I bless the long incensed gods.

I feel nature too much and the excess of my joy;

But heaven is ravishing me of the blessing it is sending me!

It is giving you to Cassander!

OLYMPIAS:

Ah! If in your flank

Olympias had drawn the source of her blood,

If I believe my love of him, if you are my mother,

Can the generous Cassander displease you?

HIGH PRIEST:

Yes, you are her blood, you cannot doubt it.

Cassander in the end admits it, he's just attested to it.

May the two of you be reunited through her

To at last conciliate the two enemy races!

OLYMPIAS:

Who? Him? Your enemy! Such will be my misfortune!

STATIRA:

He is your father Alexander's poisoner.

From the breast of Statira from whom you claim birth

In this unfortunate breast which nourished your infancy

That you just embraced for the first time,

He plunged the knife with which he struck kings.

He is pursuing me at last even to the Temple of Ephesus.

There he braves the gods while feigning to appease them!

He dares to ravish you from my maternal arms.

And you can ask if I must hate him!

OLYMPIAS:

What! Heaven sees the family of Alexander here!

What! You are his widow! Olympias is his daughter!

And your murderer, mother, is my spouse!

I am in your arms only an object of wrath!

What! This marriage so dear was a horrible crime!

HIGH PRIEST:

Hope in heaven.

OLYMPIAS:

Ah! Its inflexible hate

From which no shadow of hope can flatter my prayers,

As it opened my eyes it opened an abyss.

I see what I am and what I must be.

The greatest of my ills is actually to know myself!

On the altar that you are to unite us, I must

Expire as a victim and fall at your feet.

(A Priest enters.)

PRIEST:

They are threatening the temple and the divine mysteries

Are soon profaned by bold hands.

The two disunited kings are battling before our eyes

The right to command where the gods command.

Behold what they are announcing to these wailing vaults

And under our fearful feet our trembling dwellings.

It seems that heaven intends to inform us

That the earth is offended and must be calmed!

A people completely distracted, excited by discord,

Is rushing towards the sacred precinct and precipitating itself.

Ephesus is divided into two factions.

Soon we will resemble other nations.

Holiness, peace, morality are going to disappear;

The kings are carrying them off and we will have a master.

HIGH PRIEST:

Ah! then at least they will take their crimes far from us!

Let them leave on earth an asylum of peace!

Their interest demands it—O tender and august mother.

And you—shall I say, alas! The wife of Cassander?

You can cast yourself at the foot of these altars.

I am going to present myself to audacious kings

I know the respect that one owes to their crown.

But they owe more to this God who gives it to them.

If they intend to reign they cannot irritate him.

I know we are without arms, without soldiers.

We have only our laws, that's our power.

God alone is my support, his temple is my defense.

And if tyranny dares to approach in it,

It's over my bloody body that it must march.

(The High Priest and the Priest leave.)

STATIRA:

O destiny! O God of altars and thrones!

Against Cassander at least favor Antigonus.

My daughter, in the decline of my life, I need and

Expect help only from our enemies

And to seek an avenger in the breast of my misery

Amongst the usurpers of the throne of your father!

Amongst our own subjects, whose jealous efforts

Are disputing a hundred realms that I once possessed entirely!

They crawled at my feet, here they are my masters.

O throne of Cyrus! O blood of my ancestors!

Into what deep abyss are you descended!

Vanity of grandeur, I no longer know you.

OLYMPIAS:

My mother I am with you— Ah! In this funereal day

At least make me worthy of the great name which remains to you.

The duty that it prescribes is my only hope.

STATIRA:

Daughter of the king of kings, fulfill that duty.

CURTAIN

ACT III

The temple is closed.

CASSANDER:

Truth is getting out of hand, it's no longer time for silence.

This funereal secret which my father kept hidden

Must give way to the public clamor.

Yes, I've done justice to the daughter of kings.

Must I much longer, through a cruel silence,

Still do to her blood a mortal offense?

I am guilty enough.

SOSTERNES:

But a jealous rival

Is using the great name of Olympias against you.

He's rousing the populace; Ephesus is alarmed

The aroused fury of religion

That Antigonus scorns, he knows how to excite.

Having killed the mother, you are committing a frightful crime,

A detestable crime, to possess the daughter.

CASSANDER:

You know the bloody reproaches that Ephesus

Can make me, great God! Cannot approach mine.

Thanks to heaven, I've calmed the hearts of the citizens.

Mine will always be the victim of the furies,

The victim of love and of my barbarism.

Alas! I wanted for her to hold everything from me.

That she would be unaware of a fate that froze me with terror.

I was placing the inheritance of her father in her hands,

Conquered by Antipater, my share today.

Happy with my love, happy with my blessings,

One time in my life with myself at peace.

Everything will be redressed, I will render her justice.

After all, my heart was not the accomplice of any crime.

I killed Statira, but in battle,

It was in saving my father, that I readied my arm against her.

It's in the distraction of murder and carnage

In which a son's duty distracted my courage

It was blindness that night and horror

Spread over my troubled eyes by means of madness!

My soul shook, having been punished,

By this fatal love which holds it enslaved.

I think myself innocent in the judgment of the gods,

Before the whole world but not in my own eyes.

Not at all for Olympias, and that's my torture

That's my despair. She must choose

Whether to pardon me or pierce my heart.

This despairing heart which is burning with fury.

SOSTERNES:

They assert that Olympias, brought to this temple,

Can withdraw the hand she gave you.

CASSANDER:

Yes, Sosternes, I know it; and if by this law

The creature that I idolize is abused against me,

Bad luck to my rival, and bad luck to this temple!

Of the most holy cult I will here make an example.

I will soon turn it over to vengeance and horror.

Let's take this idle terror far from me.

I am loved; her heart was mine from infancy,

And love is the god who will take up my defense.

Let's rush to Olympias.

(The High Priest leaves the temple.)

CASSANDER:

Interpreter of heaven,

Minister of clemency, on this solemn day

I've spared your holy temple from alarms.

I still haven't taken arms against Antigonus.

I've respected these days dedicated to peace

But give that peace to my torn senses.

I have more than one right here, I shall know how to defend them.

I am dying without Olympias, and you must give her up.

Let's complete this marriage.

HIGH PRIEST:

Lord, she's performing

Very sacred duties and very dear to her heart.

CASSANDER:

All my partisans share them. Where then is the priestess

Who must offer my wife to me and bless my tenderness?

HIGH PRIEST:

She is going to bring her. Let such beautiful bonds

Not work misfortune for the two of you today!

CASSANDER:

Our misfortune! Alas! This single day

Saw the course of so many ills terminated.

For the first time a moment of sweetness

Is dissipating the darkness of my frightful pains.

HIGH PRIEST:

Perhaps Olympias is to be pitied more than you.

CASSANDER:

What do you mean? What are you saying?

Eh! What can she fear?

HIGH PRIEST:

(as he is leaving) You will learn so enough.

CASSANDER:

No, stay. Eh, what!

Are you taking part with Antigonus against me?

HIGH PRIEST:

May the heavens preserve me from passing the limits

That my peaceful cult prescribes to my zeal.

Court intrigues, the shouts of factions,

The sad passions of mortals that I am fleeing

Have not yet troubled our obscure retreats.

To the god we are serving we raise our pure hands.

The quarrels of great kings, prompt to divide them,

Are to us known only to appease them

And we would be unaware of their transient grandeurs

But for the fatal need they have for our prayers.

For you, for Olympias, and for others, Lord,

I am going to implore the favor of the immortals.

CASSANDER:

Olympias!

HIGH PRIEST:

This moment recall her to these parts.

See if you still have rights over her.

I am leaving you.

(The High Priest leaves and the temple opens.)

CASSANDER:

(As Olympias and Statira enter from the interior of the temple)

She's trembling, O heaven, and I am quaking!

What! You are lowering your tear filled eyes!

You are turning away from me that face in which nature

Depicted the most noble soul and the purest passion!

OLYMPIAS:

(throwing herself in the arms of her mother)

Ah! Barbarian!— Ah! Madame!

CASSANDER:

Explain yourself, speak.

Into whose arms are you fleeing my desolated glances?

What have they said about me? Why am I causing such alarms?

Who's this that accompanies you, and bathes you with tears?

STATIRA:

(unveiling and turning toward Cassander) See who I am.

CASSANDER:

Her features—her voice!

My blood is freezing! Where am I? And what am I seeing?

STATIRA:

Your crimes.

CASSANDER:

Statira can reappear here!

STATIRA:

Wretch! Recognize the widow of your master,

The mother of Olympias.

CASSANDER:

O heavenly thunders.

Roar over me, break over this criminal face!

STATIRA:

Why didn't you make this horrible prayer sooner?

Eternal enemy of my whole family,

If heaven wanted it, if through your first blows,

You alone made my husband and my throne collapse.

If on that day of crime, in the midst of carnage,

Barbarian, you sensed in yourself little enough courage

To strike a woman, and piercing her side

To plunge your hands in the waves of her blood,

Leave me what remains of this wretched blood.

Must your hand at all times be funeral to me?

Don't tear my daughter from my heart, from my arms;

When heaven returns her to me, don't carry her away from me.

Earthly tyrants have always separated

Respect, at least, for the asylum in which I am interred.

Wretch, don't come with unworthy efforts

To persecute the dead in these sacred tombs.

CASSANDER:

You have struck me more than thunder could have

And my face dares not touch the ground at your feet.

I confess myself unworthy after my attempted murders.

And if I excuse myself because of the horror of battles,

If I inform you that my hand was deceived

When the thread of the life of a hero was cut

That I was serving my father in arming myself against you,

I would be unable to soften your just wrath.

Nothing can excuse me. Yet I might say

That I saved this blood that my tenderness adores,

That I am placing at your feet my scepter and my realm.

All is horrifying for you! You are not listening to me!

My hand would snatch my wretched life from me

Less full of crimes than punished remorse,

If your own blood, the object of so much love,

Despite herself, despite me, didn't attach me to life.

With holy respect I raised your daughter.

I defended her for fifteen years from my father and my family.

She has my vows, my heart, and perhaps the gods

Who are assembled in this august abode

Will let the shocking horror of our fate

Be repaired through a holy marriage.

STATIRA:

What marriage! O my blood! You will receive the faith

Of whom? Of the assassin of Alexander and myself?

OLYMPIAS:

No—mother, extinguish these terrifying torches,

These torches of hymen in our guilty hands.

Extinguish in my heart the frightful memory

Of bonds, of sad bonds which must have joined us.

I prefer, and there's nothing in

This choice that should astonish you,

Ashes with which you are covered to the scepter he is giving me.

I don't hesitate; leave me in your arms

To forget love with so many crimes.

Your daughter became his accomplice by loving him.

Pardon: accept my just sacrifice.

If possible separate my heart and his misdeeds,

Especially prevent me from ever seeing him again.

STATIRA:

I recognize my daughter and am less unfortunate.

You restore a little life to my frightful languor.

I am reborn. Ah! Great gods! Did you want my hand

To present Olympias to this inhuman monster?

What were you exacting of me? What frightful ministry

Both for your priestess, alas, and for her mother!

You had pity: you didn't want it

To catch me in the snare into which you were guiding my steps.

Cruel man, don't insult the altar and the throne;

You soiled the walls of Babylon with my blood.

I would yet prefer a second time

To see that blood shed by the assassin of kings

Than to see my subject, my enemy—Cassander—

Insolently love Alexander's daughter.

CASSANDER:

I still condemn myself with greater harshness,

But I love, but give in to love in fury.

Olympia belongs to me; I know what my father did.

I am a king like him, I have the same character,

I have the same rights, the same power;

She is, in the end, my wife.

Nothing can separate my fate and her destiny.

Neither terrors, nor you, nor the gods, nor my crimes.

Nothing can ever break such legitimate fetters.

Heaven didn't turn away from my remorse.

And since it united us, it has pardoned everything.

But if they intend to separate me from this adored spouse,

Her hand which belongs to me, her faith that she swore;

They must shed this blood, they must take my heart out

Which knows nothing but her and which horrifies you.

In my eyes your altars no longer are privileged.

If I'm a murderer, I will be a sacrilegious man.

I will carry off my wife from this temple, from your arms.

From the gods themselves, from our gods,

If they won't hearken to me.

I demand death, I want it, I envy it,

But I shall not expire except as the spouse of Olympias.

Despite you, I must bear to the tomb

Both the most tender love and the finest name

And the terrible remorse of an involuntary crime

Which will at least soften the Manes of her father.

(Cassander leaves with Sosternes.)

STATIRA:

What a moment! What blasphemy! O heaven! What did I hear?

Ah! My daughter, at what price is my blood returned to me?

I can see that you resent the horrors I am experiencing.

My sorrow is found in your terrified eyes.

Your heart responds to mine. Your dear hugs,

Your enflamed sighs, console my torments.

They are less mournful when you share them.

My daughter is my asylum in this new shipwreck.

I can endure everything, because I see in you

A heart worthy indeed of Alexander and me.

OLYMPIAS:

Ah! Heaven is my witness if my soul is formed

To imitate yours, and to be animated

With the same sentiments and the same virtues.

O widow of Alexander! O blood of Darius!

My mother! Ah! Was it needful that the hands of Cassander

That robbed me from your arms raised me?

Why did your murderer, foreseeing my wishes,

Mark his life for me with benefactions?

Why has his cruel hand never oppressed me!

Benefactions too dangerous! Why has he loved me?

STATIRA:

Heavens! Who do I see appear in these retired abodes?

Antigonus himself!

ANTIGONUS:

(entering) O queen! Stay.

You see one of the kings created by Alexander

Who respects his widow and is coming to defend her.

You can climb from the foot of this altar

To the first rank of the world where heaven placed you.

Put your daughter there, and at least take vengeance.

On your haughty ravisher who is offending all three of us.

Your fate is known, all hearts are yours.

They are weary of tyrants that your august spouse

Left masters of his empire by his death.

For this great change your name can suffice.

Will you admit me here as your defender?

STATIRA:

Yes, it's pity which directs your heart,

If you serve my blood, if your offer is sincere.

ANTIGONUS:

I shall not suffer that a bold youth

From the hands of your daughter and with so many virtues

Obtain a double right to the throne of Cyrus.

He's too unworthy of it, and for such a share

I presume he doesn't have your vote.

I haven't opened my heart to the High Priest.

I am presenting myself as a worshipper

Who implores clemency of the divinities.

I am presenting myself to you armed with vengeance.

The widow of Alexander, forgetting her grandeur,

Will not, at least, forget honor of her family to such a degree.

STATIRA:

My heart is detached from the throne and from life.

The first was stolen from me, the second soon finished.

But if you snatch from the hands of a ravisher

The only treasure the gods have given to my sorrow,

If you protect her, if you avenge her father,

I will no longer see in you anything but my tutelary god.

Lord, save my daughter, by the edge of my tomb,

From the crime and the danger of marrying my executioner.

ANTIGONUS:

Worthy blood of Alexander, do you approve my zeal?

Do you accept my offer and think like she does?

OLYMPIAS:

I ought to hate Cassander.

ANTIGONUS:

I must be granted

The prize, the noble prize that I am coming to demand.

Against my ally I am taking your defense.

I think to deserve you: be my reward.

Everything else is an outrage, and it's you I want.

Cassander wasn't made to obtain your vows.

Speak, and my arm will uphold

Of the queen, and especially of you yourself.

Pronounce: do you deign to honor me with such a prize?

STATIRA:

Decide.

OLYMPIAS:

Let me get my wits about me.

I am hardly opening my eyes. Trembling, shocked,

Hurled from the breast of slavery in this temple.

Daughter of Statira, daughter of a demi-god,

I find a mother in this august place.

Despoiled of his name, his rank and his treasure

And from a deadly sleep hardly awakened;

I marry a benefactor—he is an assassin.

My spouse cut up my mother's breast.

In this heap of horrible adventures

You offer me your hand to avenge my injuries.

What can I reply to you?— Ah! In such moments— (hugging her mother)

You see to whom I owe my first feelings.

See if the torch of nuptial celebrations

Is made to light these fatal horrors.

What crowd of ills surround me in a single day,

And if this frozen heart could listen to love.

STATIRA:

Ah! I will respond to you for her,

And heaven is giving her to you.

The majesty or perhaps the pride of my throne

Hadn't destined, in my original plans,

The daughter of Alexander for one of my subjects.

But you deserve her by daring to defend her.

It was you that expiring Alexander designated.

He named the most worthy, and you've become it.

His throne is your treasure if you sustain it.

May the favor of the immortal gods second you!

May their hand lead you to the empire of the world!

Alexander and his widow, both enslaved,

He in the tomb and I in these shadowy walls,

Will see you without regret on the throne of my fathers,

And may fate, henceforth less severe,

Protect you from this fatality

Which always overturns this embloodied throne!

ANTIGONUS:

It will be raised up by the hand of Olympias.

Show yourself with her to the people of Asia.

Leave this refuge, and I am going to urge all

To avenge Alexander and to replace him.

(Exit Antigonus.)

STATIRA:

My daughter, it's through you that I am breaking the barrier

That separates me here from all of nature.

In a moment I am returning to this perverse world

To avenge my spouse, your marriage and your fetters.

God will give strength to my maternal hands

To smash with you your criminal chains.

Come fulfill my promise and make me forget

By new oaths, the crime of the first.

OLYMPIAS:

Alas!

STATIRA:

What! You lament?

OLYMPIAS:

This same day

To light the marriage torches twice?

STATIRA:

What are you saying?

OLYMPIAS:

Allow me, for the first time

To make you hear a timid voice.

I cherish you, my mother, and I want to pour out

The blood that I received from you and Alexander

If I obtain from the gods by shedding it

The prolongation of your days or their consolation.

STATIRA:

O my darling Olympias!

OLYMPIAS:

Dare I still say

That your obscure asylum is the throne to which I aspire?

You will see me submissive there and crushing at your feet

These wretched thrones, by you alone forgotten.

My father Alexander, shut in his tomb,

Does he want that his enemy succumb by our hands?

Let's leave that to these kings in the horror of battles,

To punish one by means of the other and to avenge his death.

But as for us, of so many ills the innocent victims

To their frantic arms join our trembling hands,

Must we take on ourselves a fruitless murder?

Tears are for us, crimes are for them.

STATIRA:

Tears! And for whom do I see them shed here?

Gods! Have you rendered me the daughter of Alexander?

Is it she that I hear?

OLYMPIAS:

Mother—

STATIRA:

O vengeful heaven!

OLYMPIAS:

Cassander!

STATIRA:

Explain yourself; you are freezing me with horror.

Speak.

OLYMPIAS:

I cannot.

STATIRA:

Go, you are tearing out my soul.

End this terrible trouble; speak, I say.

OLYMPIAS:

Ah! Madame,

I feel too much the blows I've just struck you with.

But I cherish you too deeply to wish to deceive you.

Prepared to separate myself from a spouse so guilty,

I am fleeing him—but I love him.

STATIRA:

O execrable word!

Last of my life! Cruel daughter, alas!

Because you love him, you won't flee him.

You love him! You are betraying Alexander and your mother!

Great God! I've seen my husband and my father perish.

You are tearing my daughter from me, and your inhuman decree

Makes me find her again only to die by her hand,

OLYMPIAS:

I am throwing myself at your feet.

STATIRA:

Unnatural daughter!

Daughter too dear!

OLYMPIAS:

Alas, by sorrows devoured

Trembling at your knees, I am bathing them with tears.

Mother, forgive—

STATIRA:

I forgive and I am dying.

OLYMPIAS:

Live, listen to me.

STATIRA:

What do you want?

OLYMPIAS:

I swear to you

By the gods, by my name, by you, by nature,

That I will punish myself for it, that Olympias today

Will shed all her blood before belonging to him.

My heart is known to you. I told you that I love;

Judge by my weakness, and even by this confession,

If this heart belongs to you and you are bearing it away

From my distracted sense that love has tamed.

Don't consider my weakness and my age;

From my father and from you I feel my courage.

I've been able to offend, I cannot betray;

And you will know me in seeing me die.

STATIRA:

You can die, you say, inhuman and beloved daughter,

And you cannot hate the assassin of your father.

OLYMPIAS:

Tear my heart out, you will see that a spouse,

However dear he was to me, reigns in it less than you.

You will recognize in it this pure blood that animates me.

To justify yourself, take your victim.

Immolate your daughter.

STATIRA:

Ah! I trust in your virtues.

I pity you Olympias, and I do not accuse you.

I hope in your duty, I hope in your courage.

As for myself, I was pitied by a love that outrages me.

You are tearing my heart apart and you know how to soften it.

Console your mother at least by making her die.

Go, I am wretched and you are not guilty.

OLYMPIAS:

O heaven! Which of us is the most miserable?

CURTAIN

ACT IV

In the peristyle.

HERMAS:

You indeed told me, the holy places profaned

With the horrors of battles are going to be abandoned.

Your soldiers near the temple are occupying this passage.

Cassander, intoxicated by love, by sorrow, by rage,

Defying the wrath of the very gods he invokes,

Is advancing against you by this other path.

The signal is given; but in this enterprise

The populace is divided between you and Cassander.

ANTIGONUS:

(leaving) I will reunite them.

CASSANDER:

(blocking Antigonus) Stay, unworthy friend,

Unfaithful ally, detestable enemy,

Are you daring to contest with me what heaven is giving me?

ANTIGONUS:

Yes.

Where's the surprise in which your heart's abandoning itself?

The daughter of Alexander has rights great enough

To make Asia rise in arms and make our tyrants tremble.

Babylon is her dowry, and the empire is her right.

I pretend to both; and I really mean to tell you

That your tears, you regrets, your expiations,

Will not impose on the eyes of the people

Even if you were made innocent of the death of the father

Don't think that now friendship is so regarded

Opinion makes everything; it condemns you.

To the weaknesses of love your abandoned heart

Seduced Olympias by hiding her birth.

You thought to enshroud in eternal silence

This funereal secret of which I am informed.

It's not by deceiving her that you can be loved.

Her eyes are finally opened, and it is done; and Cassander

Dares not raise his, having no more right to pretend.

With what are you flattering yourself?

Do you think that her rights

Will raise you one day to the rank of king of kings?

I can take the defense of Statira here.

But do you want to preserve our long alliance?

Do you want to reign in peace in your new Realm?

To see me friend again, to support you with my arm?

CASSANDER:

Well?

ANTIGONUS:

Give up Olympias, and nothing separates us.

I will perish for you: if not I declare to you

That I am the greatest of all your enemies.

Know your interests, weigh them, and choose.

CASSANDER:

I won't have any trouble and I came to make you

A different offer, and which might please you.

You know neither law, nor remorse, nor pity.

And it's a game for you to betray friendship.

I, at least, fear heaven: you laugh at its justice.

You enjoy crimes of which I made you the accomplice.

You won't rejoice in them, traitor—

ANTIGONUS:

What do you intend?

CASSANDER:

If in your atrocious soul there is some virtue

Let's not employ the hands of mercenary soldiers

To glut your rage and serve my wrath.

What have the populace in common with our factions?

Is it for them to die for our squabbles?

It's for us, it's for you, if you feel the audacity

To brave my courage, as well as my disgrace.

I was not admitted to communication with the gods

To go slaughter my friend under their eyes.

It's a new crime; it's you who are preparing it.

Go, we were made to be barbarians.

Let's march; come decide your fate and mine,

To drink my blood or pour out yours.

ANTIGONUS:

I consent to it with joy; and be sure that Olympias

Will accept the hand which separates you from life.

(They draw their swords. The High Priest emerges from the temple precipitously with priests and initiates who hurl themselves with a crowd of people between Cassander and Antigonus and disarm them.)

HIGH PRIEST:

Profane ones, this is too much. Stop, respect

The god who speaks to you and his solemnities.

Priests, initiates, people, let them be separated.

Banish from this holy place barbarous discord.

Expiate your crimes— Swords, vanish.

Powerful God, pardon! You, kings, obey.

CASSANDER:

I give in to heaven, to you.

ANTIGONUS:

I persist: and I call as witness

The Manes of Alexander, and the celestial wrath.

So long as I live I won't suffer

That Olympias pass into his arms before my eyes,

And that this illegitimate, impious marriage

Shall be the shame of Ephesus and the horror of Asia.

CASSANDER:

No question it will be if you had created it.

HIGH PRIEST:

With a mind more resigned, with a heart less inflamed,

Give up to the law, respect its justice.

It's common to both of you, it must be accomplished.

The hut of the poor and the throne of kings

Equally submit, hearing this voice.

It aids the weak, it is the curb of crime

And frees at the altar the innocent victim.

If the spouse, whoever he may be and whatever may be his rank,

Has shed the blood of his wife's relations,

He must be purified in our sacred mysteries

By the fires of Vesta and the healthy waters

And by repentance more necessary than those.

His spouse in one day can form other bonds.

She can do so without shame, at least if her clemency

Through the example of the gods, does not pardon the offense.

The law gives her a single day: she can shorten the time

Of the pain attached to these great changes

But especially await the orders of a mother.

She has resumed her rights, the sacred character

That nature gives, and that nothing weakens.

To her august voice Olympias is obedient.

What can you dare to attempt, when it's up to you to await

The decrees of the widow of Alexander?

(He leaves with his followers.)

ANTIGONUS:

That's enough, I subscribe to it, pontiff: she is mine.

(Antigonus leaves with Hermas.)

CASSANDER:

She won't be of a barbarous and faithless heart.

Sosternes, let's snatch her from this fatal asylum,

From the insolent pretension of this guilty cynic

Who laughs at my remorse, insults my sorrow

And, tranquil and serene, comes to tear my heart out.

SOSTERNES:

He seduced Statira, Lord; he's acting on authority

Of both the laws he's violating and the gods that he scorns.

CASSANDER:

Let's carry her off, I tell you, to the gods that I have served

And by whom, henceforth, all my efforts are betrayed.

I will accept death, I will bless the lightning.

But in the end if my spouse dares to decide

To pass, in one day, here at this fatal altar

From the hand of Cassander to the hand of a rival!

Let this temple fall in ashes before I endure that!

Heaven! You will forgive me. More calm and more pure

My soul dares to abandon itself to this hope.

You are separating me from Olympias, is it to pardon her?

SOSTERNES:

It isn't separating you at all: this tender and docile heart

So submissive to your sway, so happy to surrender itself,

Cannot pass to forgetfulness in a moment.

The heart cannot make such a prompt change.

She can love you without betraying nature.

Your blows in battle carried by chance

Have spilled, I confess, a very precious blood.

It's a misfortune that the gods allow you.

You didn't soak in the blood of her father.

Your tears have effaced all the blood of her mother.

Her misfortunes are passed, your blessings are present.

CASSANDER:

Idly this idea appeases my torments.

This blood of Statira, these Manes of Alexander,

Are making themselves heard here with a very terrible voice.

Sosternes, she is their daughter, she has the frightful right

To hate unchangeably a wretched spouse.

I feel that she abhors me, and as for me, I prefer her

To the throne of Cyrus, to the throne of the world.

These expiations, these hidden mysteries

Indifferent to kings and sought out again by me,

She was the object of it; my criminal soul

Approached the gods only so as to approach her.

SOSTERNES:

(noticing Olympias)

Alas! Behold her in prey to her sorrows.

She's embracing an altar and bathing it with tears.

CASSANDER:

From the temple, from this altar, it's time I carried her off.

Go, hurry, let everything be prepared.

(Sosternes leaves.)

OLYMPIAS:

(bent over the altar without seeing Cassander)

How my heart is soothed.

How desperate it is! How it condemns itself! Alas! (noticing Cassander)

What do I see?

CASSANDER:

Your husband.

OLYMPIAS:

No, you are not.

No, Cassander—never pretend to be.

CASSANDER:

Well! I am unworthy to be, and I ought to know myself.

I know all the crimes that my inhuman fate

Has committed by my hand to ruin the two of us.

I thought to expiate them, I am filling the measure with them.

My presence is a crime, and my passion an insult

But deign to reply to me—did I by my help

Tear your life from the furors of war?

OLYMPIAS:

Why conserve it?

CASSANDER:

From childhood

Have I respected your sweet innocence?

Have I idolized you?

OLYMPIAS:

Ah! There's my misfortune.

CASSANDER:

After the tender confession of the most pure passion,

Free in your goodness, mistress of yourself,

This favorable voice to the husband who loves you,

In the place where I am speaking to you, at these same altars,

Joined my oaths to your solemn oaths!

OLYMPIAS:

Alas! It is too true—May the celestial wrath

Not punish me for such a funereal oath.

CASSANDER:

You love me, Olympias!

OLYMPIAS:

Ah! To complete the horror

Don't reproach me for my detestable error.

It was very easy to dazzle my youth.

You knew the weakness of a heart which was ignorant.

It's one crime the more. Flee me, these conversations

Are a more frightful crime for me than for you.

CASSANDER:

Beware committing a more funereal one, perhaps

By accepting the vows of a barbarian and a traitor.

And if for Antigonus—

OLYMPIAS:

Stop, wretch!

I reject the vows of Antigonus and you.

After this hand, cowardly abused,

Was able to join to your hand my sprinkled blood,

No mortal, henceforth, will have rights over my heart.

I hold marriage, and the world and life, in horror.

Mistress of my choice, without deliberating

I am choosing the tomb in which my mother is shut.

I choose this asylum where god must possess

This heart which deceived itself when it gave in to you.

I embrace the altars and I detest your throne

And all those of Asia—and especially that of Antigonus.

Go away, never see me again—Go, leave me to weep

Over the love I pledged and must abhor.

CASSANDER:

Well! if the love of my rival offends you

You won't separate me from a ray of hope.

And when your virtue rejects another spouse

This refusal is mercy to me and I believe in you.

Soiled though I am with the blood of she who gave you birth

You are, you will be the better half of my being,

The dearest and holy half, and whose virtues

Have halted the lightning suspended over me

Have taken a supreme sway over my heart

And ought to disarm your mother herself.

OLYMPIAS:

My mother! What! Your mouth pronounced her name.

Ah! If repentance, if compassion,

If your love, at least, could soften your audacity,

Flee these parts where she dwells,

And the altar that I am embracing.

Leave me alone.

CASSANDER:

No, I don't know how to leave without you.

You must consent to follow me instantly. (taking her by the hand)

Dear wife, come.

OLYMPIAS:

(pulling away, distracted) Treat me then like her;

Strike an unfortunate faithful to her duty.

Into this desolated heart bring a more certain blow;

All my blood was made to spill under your hand.

Strike, I say.

CASSANDER:

Ah! Very far from bearing you vengeance,

I had less cruelty, I had less violence.

Heaven knows how to be merciful, and you to punish.

But it's too much to be an ingrate, and it's too much to hate me.

OLYMPIAS:

Is my hate just and have you deserved it?

Cassander, if your ferocious embloodied hand,

Your hand which dared to pierce my mother's flank,

Had struck only me, and shed only my blood,

I would pardon you, I would love you—barbarian.

Go away, everything separates us.

CASSANDER:

No, nothing is separating us.

Even if you were to hold Cassander in greater horror,

Even if you married me to pierce my heart,

You will follow me. My fate must be accomplished.

Leave me my love, at least for my punishment.

This punishment is without end, and I swear it by you.

Hate, punish, but follow your husband.

(Enter Sosternes.)

SOSTERNES:

Appear, or soon Antigonus is carrying her off.

He's speaking to your warriors, he's besieging the gate,

He's seducing your friends assembled near the temple

With his formidable voice; they seem disturbed.

He calls to witness Alexander, he calls to witness Olympias.

Tremble for your love, tremble for your life.

Come.

CASSANDER:

Thus you are sacrificing me to my rival!

I am going to seek death since you wish it.

OLYMPIAS:

Me, wish your death!—get out, I'm incapable of it.

Live far from me.

CASSANDER:

Without you, life is execrable to me.

And if it's preserved to me, I am returning to this place.

I will tear you from the temple, or die there before your eyes.

(He leaves with Sosternes.)

OLYMPIAS:

Wretched woman! And it's he who is causing my alarms!

Ah! Cassander, is it up to you to cost me tears?

Must there be so many battles to fulfill duty?

You would have an absolute power over my soul,

O blood from which I was born, o voice of nature!

I am abandoning myself to you, it's for you that I am swearing

To sacrifice to you my dearest feelings.

On this altar, alas! I took other oaths.

Gods! You received them! O gods! Your clemency

Ought to approve the innocence of the most tender love.

You've changed everything—well then change my heart.

Give it the virtue conforming to its misfortune.

Have some pity on a torn soul

Which is perishing unfaithful or dying unnatural.

Alas! I was happy in my obscurity,

In the forgetfulness of mankind, in captivity;

Without parents, without rank, unknown even to myself.

The great name that I bear is what has ruined me.

At least I will be worthy of it—Cassander I must flee you,

I must abandon you—but how can I hate you?

What power does a weak mortal have over itself?

I am tearing at my cruel wound, weeping,

And this unfortunate dart that my hand seeks

I push into my heart instead of tearing it out.

(The High Priest, priests, and priestesses enter.)

OLYMPIAS:

Pontiff, where are you hurrying? Protect my weakness.

You are trembling, you are weeping!

HIGH PRIEST:

Unfortunate princess!

I am weeping for your situation.

OLYMPIAS:

Ah! Be its support.

HIGH PRIEST:

Resign yourself to heaven—you have nothing but that.

OLYMPIAS:

Alas! What are you saying?

HIGH PRIEST:

O dear and august daughter,

The widow of Alexander—

OLYMPIAS:

Ah! Just gods!—my mother!

Well—

HIGH PRIEST:

All is lost. The two furious kings,

Trampling on the laws, armed against the gods,

Into the sanctuary of the sacred enclosure

Encouraged their troops readied for murder.

Already spilling blood, swords in hand,

Cassander to you was beating a path.

I marched against him, having for my defense

Only the laws he was forgetting;

And our gods that he is offending.

Your distracted mother, offered herself to his blows.

Thinking herself master at once of the temple and you,

Weary of horrors, weary of so many crimes,

She seized the sword that strikes sacrifices

Plunging it into this flank where irritated heaven

Made you draw life and calamity.

OLYMPIAS:

(falling into the arms of a priestess)

I am dying—support me—let's march— Is she still living?

HIGH PRIEST:

Cassander is at her feet: he laments, he implores

He still dares to ready his funereal aid

To innocent hands which are reviving her life.

He shrieks out on himself, he accuses himself,

He throws his weapons far away.

OLYMPIAS:

(rising) Cassander at her knees!

HIGH PRIEST:

He's bathing them with tears.

To his cries, to our voices, she rolls her eyes.

She sees in him only an audacious monster

Who's tearing from her the remains of her life.

By this funereal hand pursued at all times

Weak, and sustaining herself by a final effort,

She falls, she's reaching the moment of death.

She abhors, at the same time, Cassander and life

And raising regretfully her debilitated eyelids,

"Go," she said to me, "Unfortunate minister

Of an unlucky temple profaned by blood.

Console Olympias. She loves me, and I direct

That to avenge her mother, she marry Antigonus."

OLYMPIAS:

Let's go die beside her. Exact from me, great gods!

Come, guide my steps, come shut our eyes.

HIGH PRIEST:

Arm yourself with courage; he must appear here.

OLYMPIAS:

Lord, I have need of it, and perhaps, I will have some.

CURTAIN

ACT V

HERMAS:

Pity must speak and vengeance is vain;

An unlucky rival is not worthy of hate.

Flee this funereal place: today, Lord,

Olympias will be lost for you and for him.

ANTIGONUS:

What! Statira is no more!

HERMAS:

It's Cassander's fate

To be forever fatal to the great name of Alexander.

Statira, succumbing to the weight of her sorrows,

Expired with horror in the arms of her daughter.

The sensitive Olympias, stretched at her feet,

Felt her painfully retained soul exhale.

The ministers of the gods, the priestesses in tears

Mixing in their regrets increased their sorrows.

Cassander, shocked, feels all their seizures.

The temple is echoing with outbursts and complaints.

They are preparing a funeral pyre, and these vain decorations

Which recall the dead to the sight of the living.

They pretend that Olympias, in this solitary place,

Will live in the asylum that entombed her mother.

That from the world, from marriage, tearing her beautiful life,

She will consecrate to the gods their deplorable court.

And that she must weep in eternal silence

For her family, her mother and even her birth.

ANTIGONUS:

No, no, she must follow the laws of her duty.

In the end, I have over her irrevocable rights.

Statira gave her to me, and her supreme orders

At the moment of death are the laws of the gods themselves.

This frantic Cassander and his funeral passion

Caused a just horror to the blood of Statira.

HERMAS:

Lord, you believe that?

ANTIGONUS:

She herself declared

That her desolated heart renounced this barbarian.

If he still dares to love her, I've promised his death.

I'll keep my word and you mustn't doubt it.

HERMAS:

Would you mix blood to the tears you see shed,

To the flames of the funeral pyre, to these august ashes?

Struck by a holy respect, know that your soldiers

Are recoiling with horror and will not follow you.

ANTIGONUS:

No, I cannot be troubled by funerary pomps.

I've taken an oath; Cassander reveres her.

I know the laws that I must respect;

That to win the populace I must imitate them.

Avenger of Statira, Protector of Olympias,

I must here be the example of the rest of Asia.

Everything speaks in my favor, and my delayed blows

Will have the more force for it and be more certain.

(The temple opens.)

(Antigonus, Hermas, the High Priest, the priests slowly come forward; Olympias is in mourning supported by the priestesses.)

HERMAS:

They are leading Olympias hardly breathing.

I see emerging from the temple the august high priest

Who dampens with his tears the tracks of his steps.

The priestesses of the gods are holding her in their arms.

ANTIGONUS:

These objects would touch the heart of the most ferocious.

(to Olympias) I really mean to admit it.—All know that my mouth,

In mixing my regrets with your sad sighs,

Swears again to avenge so many frightful annoyances.

The enemy who twice deprived you of a mother

Nourishes in his furor a bold hope.

Know that all is ready for his punishment

Don't add fear to your affliction

Be secure against his attempts.

OLYMPIAS:

Ah! Lord, speak less of murder and vengeance

She lived—I am dying to the rest of mortals.

ANTIGONUS:

I deplore her loss as much as I pity you.

I could recall her sacred will

So dear to my hope and revered by you.

But I know what one owes in this first moment

To her shade, to her daughter, to your despair.

Consult yourself, madame, and keep her promise.

(He leaves with Hermas.)

OLYMPIAS:

You who reckon the horror which urges me,

You, minister of a god of peace and gentleness,

The only consoler of unfortunate hearts,

Can't I, under your eyes, consecrate my misery

To water the altars with tears for my mother?

Would you really, lord, have the harshness

To shut this asylum to my calamity?

It's the unique inheritance of the blood of so many kings

Don't envy me it; leave me my share.

HIGH PRIEST:

I am weeping over your fate; but what can I do for you?

Your mother named your spouse as she died.

You heard her last will,

While with our hands we shut her eyes,

And if you resist her dying voice,

Cassander is your master, he will resume all his rights.

OLYMPIAS:

I admit it, I swore it to dying Statira

To avert my hand from that bloody hand;

I am keeping my oath.

HIGH PRIEST:

Free still in these abodes,

Your hand depends only on you and the gods.

Soon everything's going to change; you can, Olympias,

Direct now the fate of your life.

No question, one must not the same day light

Funeral pyres of the dead and the torches of love.

This mixture is terrible: but a word can suffice

And I will await this word without daring to prescribe it.

In these extremities, it's up to you to feel

What your heart owes to the blood from which you spring.

OLYMPIAS:

Lord, I've told you: this marriage and all others

Are horrible to my heart and ought to be displeasing to yours.

I don't wish to betray these incensed Manes.

I am abandoning a spouse—that's obedience enough.

Let me flee marriage, and love, and a throne.

HIGH PRIEST:

You must follow Cassander or choose Antigonus,

These two armed heroes, so proud and so jealous

Are forced now to be reconciled to you.

With one word you will become trouble and carnage

Whose shocking image our eyes will see.

Without the deep respect that inspires mortals

This apparel of death, this funeral pyre, these altars,

And these last duties, and these supreme honors,

Piety is wearying, and especially amongst the great

I have with difficulty stopped torrents of blood.

But as soon as tomorrow, this blood is going to flow in Ephesus.

Decide, princess, and appease the people.

This populace, which is always on the side of the laws,

When you have spoken, will sustain your choice.

If not, sword in hand, in this temple, in front of my sight

Cassander, reclaiming the oath he received

From a treasure he possessed, has the right to take it away

Despite the just horror he seems to inspire you with.

OLYMPIAS:

It suffices; I conceive your reasons and your fears.

I won't get carried away with any more useless complaints.

I submit to my destiny; you see its rigor.

I must make a choice—it's made in my heart.

I am determined.

HIGH PRIEST:

So then, it's Antigonus.

You are accepting the vows and the hand that he is giving you?

OLYMPIAS:

Lord, whatever it may be, perhaps this moment

Isn't made to conclude such an engagement.

You yourself admit it; and this last hour

In which my mother lived must occupy me completely.

You are going to bring her to the awaiting pyre?

HIGH PRIEST:

We must acquit ourselves of these sad duties.

An urn will contain her mortal remains.

You will gather them up.

OLYMPIAS:

Her criminal daughter

Caused her death—this daughter, at least,

Still owes some cares to her vengeful Manes.

HIGH PRIEST:

I am going to prepare everything.

OLYMPIAS:

By your laws that I am ignorant of,

Can I still see her on this blazing bed?

Can I approach this funeral apparatus?

Can I water her funeral pyre with my tears?

HIGH PRIEST:

Alas! You ought to do it; we share your tears.

You have nothing to fear; and these rivals in arms

Won't be able to trouble these sorrowful duties.

Present your perfumes, your veils, your hair

And the pure and sad offering of libations.

(The priestesses place all this around an altar.)

OLYMPIAS:

It's the unique favor that her daughter demands.

(to the inferior priestess) You who led her into this region of death,

Who shared fifteen years the horrors of her fate,

Go, return to warn me when these beloved ashes

Will be ready to fall in the flaming ditch.

May my last duties, since they are permitted to me,

Satisfy her shade—It's necessary.

PRIESTESS:

I obey.

(She leaves.)

OLYMPIAS:

(to the High Priest) Go then; raise this fatal pile,

Prepare the cypress and the sepulchral pyre,

Make the two cruel rivals come here.

I intend to explain myself at the foot of the altar,

At the aspect of my mother, before the eyes of these priestesses,

Witnesses of my misfortunes, witnesses of my promises.

My feelings, my choice will be declared.

You will pity them, perhaps, and approve them.

HIGH PRIEST:

You are still the mistress of your fate

You have only today, it's fleeing, and time presses.

(He leaves with the priests.)

OLYMPIAS:

(on the forestage, the Priestesses form a half circle around her)

O you, who in my heart at this decision resolved,

Usurped to my shame an absolute power

Which triumphs still with dying Statira,

Of Alexander in the tomb, of their trembling daughter,

Of the earth and the heavens conjured against you,

Reign, unfortunate lover, over my shredded senses.

If you love me, alas! If I dare still to believe it,

Go, you will pay very dearly for your funereal victory.

(Enter Cassander.)

CASSANDER:

Well! I am coming to fulfill my duty and your vows.

My blood must water this wretched funeral pyre.

Accept my death, it's my only hope;

Let it be with pity rather than with vengeance.

OLYMPIAS:

Cassander!

CASSANDER:

Sacred creature! Darling wife!—

OLYMPIAS:

Ah! Cruel!

CASSANDER:

There's no more pardon for this great criminal.

Unfortunate slave of fate that guides me,

My destiny is at all times to be a parricide. (throwing himself on his knees)

But I am your husband; but despite his crimes,

This husband adores you even more than ever.

Respect, while abhorring me, this marriage that I call in witness.

In the whole universe, Cassander alone remains to you.

Death is the only god who can separate us.

Perishing, I wish to see you and adore you.

Avenge yourself, punish me, but don't be a perjurer.

Go, marriage is still more holy than nature.

OLYMPIAS:

Rise, and stop profaning, at least,

These fatal ashes and my funereal duties.

When on this frightful pyre whose ignited flames

Consume the members of my mother in these parts,

Don't soil these gifts that I must present.

Don't approach, Cassander and know to listen to me.

(Enter Antigonus.)

ANTIGONUS:

Still your virtue can no longer defend itself from him.

Statira dictated to you the decree you must render.

I've respected the dead on this day of terror.

You can judge of it, since my vengeful arm

Has not yet inundated this asylum with blood

Because, still docile to your orders,

I take you in these parts for his judge and mine.

Pronounce our verdict, and fear nothing.

You will be seen, madame, at least I hope it,

To distinguish the assassin from the avenger of a mother.

Nature has some rights. Statira in the heavens,

Beside Alexander, rests her eyes here.

You are still shrouded in this temple.

But earth and heaven are observing Olympias.

You must decide between the two of us.

OLYMPIAS:

I consent to it; but I intend that you respect me.

You see these preparations, these gifts that I must make

To our infernal gods, to the Manes of a mother.

You chose this time, impetuous rivals,

To speak to me of marriage amidst tombs!

Swear to me only, soldiers of my kingly father,

Kings after his death, that if I am dear to you

In this moment at least, recognize my laws.

You will not further trouble my duties and my choice.

CASSANDER:

I must, I swear it, and you must know

How much I respect you and disdain this traitor.

ANTIGONUS:

Yes, I swear it, too, very confident your heart

Is pierced with horror of this barbarous rival.

Pronounce:

I subscribe to it.

OLYMPIAS:

Think, whatever it may cost,

You yourself said it, that Alexander is listening to me.

ANTIGONUS:

Decide before him.

CASSANDER:

I await your will.

OLYMPIAS:

Know then this heart that you are persecuting

And yourselves judge of the share that remains to me.

Whatever choice I make it must be funereal to me.

You feel all the excess of my calamity.

Learn more; know that I deserved it.

I've betrayed my parents, when I was able to know them,

I brought death to her who made me born.

I found a mother in this place of terror,

She died in my arms, she died for me.

She told her daughter, desolated at her feet:

"Marry Antigonus, and I will die consoled."

She was expiring, and I, to finish her off,

I refused.

ANTIGONUS:

In this way you can brave me,

Outrage your mother, and betray nature!

OLYMPIAS:

To her Manes, to you, I am doing no further injury.

I render justice to all and I'm rendering it to myself.

Cassander, before him, I pledged you my faith.

See if our bonds have been legitimate.

I allow you to judge; you know your crimes

It would be superfluous to reproach you for them.

Repair them one day.

CASSANDER:

I cannot touch you!

I cannot soften this horror that presses you!

OLYMPIAS:

You must be enlightened; keep your promise.

(The temple opens, the funeral pyre can be seen aflame.)

THE INFERIOR PRIESTESS:

Princess, it is time.

OLYMPIAS:

(to Cassander) See this frightful spectacle.

Cassander, at this moment, pity yourself if you can.

Contemplate this pyre, contemplate these ashes,

Recall my fetters, recall Alexander,

There's his widow, speak and say what I must do.

CASSANDER:

Sacrifice me.

OLYMPIAS:

You fate is dictated by your voice.

Await mine here. (she climbs on the platform of the altar which is near the pyre; the priestesses present her their offerings)

You, Manes of my mother,

Manes to whom I render these funerary duties,

You, that a just wrath must still animate,

You will receive gifts which may calm you.

They are perhaps worthy of my father and of you.

You, husband of Olympias, and who ought never to be,

You, who protect me with a cruel assistance,

You, through whom I lost the author of my life,

You, who cherished me so much, and for whom my weakness

Felt the tenderness of a more fatal love,

You think my cowardly passion banished from my soul—

Know (silence) that I adore you (silence)

And that I'm punishing myself for it.

Ahes of Statira, receive Olympias.

(Olympias strikes herself and throws herself into the flames.)

ALL:

Heaven!

(The High Priest and the priests and priestesses express their astonishment and consternation.)

CASSANDER:

(running to the pyre) Olympias!

THE PRIESTS:

O heaven!

ANTIGONUS:

O unheard of mania!

CASSANDER:

She is no more and all our efforts are vain. (returning to the peristyle)

Is this enough, great gods? My execrable hands

Made my king perish, his widow and my spouse!

Antigonus, is your soul still jealous?

Unfeeling witness of this horrible death,

Do you still envy the sweetness of my fate?

If your great heart is irritated by my happiness,

Share it, trust me, take this sword and imitate me.

(Kills himself.)

HIGH PRIEST:

Stop! O holy temple! O just and vengeful god!

In what profane palace have you seen more horror?

ANTIGONUS:

Thus Alexander, and his whole family,

Successors, murderers, all are ashes and dust!

Gods, whose wrath the whole world endures,

Masters of vile mortals, why did you create them?

What did Statira do? What did Olympias do?

For what are you reserving my deplorable life?

CURTAIN

THE TEMPLE OF GLORY
AN OPERA IN FIVE ACTS

CAST OF CHARACTERS

SINGING CHARACTERS in all the choruses

On the side of the King:

Eight women and sixteen men

On the side of the Queen:

Eight women and sixteen men

Bagpipes, oboes, bassoons

SINGING CHARACTERS IN ACT I

Envy

Apollo

The Nine Muses

Demons in the entourage of Envy

Demigods and Heroes in the entourage of Apollo

DANCING CHARACTERS IN ACT I

Eight demons

Seven heroes

The Nine Muses

SINGING CHARACTERS IN ACT II

Lidia

Arsine (her confidant)

Shepherds and Shepherdesses

Belus

Captive Kings and Soldiers in the train of Belus:

Apollo

The Nine Muses

DANCING CHARACTERS IN ACT II

Shepherds and Shepherdesses

SINGING CHARACTERS IN ACT III

High Priest of Glory

Priestess

Chorus of Priests and Priestesses of Glory

Warrior follower of Bacchus

Bacchante

Bacchus

Erigone

Warriors, Egyptians, Bacchantes and Satyrs in the entourage of Bacchus

DANCING CHARACTERS IN ACT III

FIRST BALLET:

Five Priestesses of Glory

Four Heroies

SECOND BALLET:

Nine Bacchantes

Six Egyptians

Eight Satyrs

SINGING CHARACTERS IN ACT IV

Plautina

Junia

Confidants of Plautina

Fania

Priests of Mars and Priestesses of Venus

Trajan

Warriors in Trajan's entourage

Six Conquered Kings in Trajan's train

Male and Female Romans

Glory

Followers of Glory

DANCING CHARACTERS IN ACT IV

FIRST BALLET:

Four Priests of Mars

Priestess of Venus

SECOND BALLET:

Followers of Glory, five men and four women

SINGING CHARACTERS IN ACT V

Roman Girl

Shepherds and Shepherdesses

Roman

Young Romans of both sexes

All the Characters of the Fourth Act

DANCING CHARACTERS IN ACT V

Romans

FIRST QUADRILLE:

Three men and two women

SECOND QUADRILLE:

Three men and two women

THIRD QUADRILLE:

Three women and two men

FOURTH QUADRILLE:

Three women and two men

ACT I

The stage represents the Cave of Envy. Through the opening of the cave can be seen a portion of the Temple of Glory, which is in the background, and the cradles of the Muses which are in the wings.

Envy enters followed by servants, torch in hand.

ENVY:

Deep abyss of Tenare

Frightful night, eternal night

Gods of forgetfulness, gods of Tartarus,

Eclipse the day that shines on me

Demons, bring me your barbarous aid

Against the God who is pursuing me.

The Muses and Glory have erected their temple

In these peaceable parts;

With what horror do I contemplate them.

How their dazzle hurts my eyes.

Deep abyss of Tenare

Frightful night, eternal night

Eclipse the day that shines on me.

Demons, bring me your barbarous aid

Against the god who pursues me.

ENVY'S ENTOURAGE:

Our glory is to destroy.

Our fate is to injure.

We are going to overthrow these frightful monuments.

Our redoubtable blows

Are more inevitable

Than the features of death and the power of time.

ENVY:

Hasten to avenge my outrage.

Muses that I hate encircle the grove.

Destroy under these foundations

Both Glory and her temple and her happy children

That I hate yet more.

Demons, enemies of the living

Present this spectacle to my fury.

(The followers of Envy dance and form a ballet figure; a hero comes into the midst of these furies, astonished at his approach, he sees himself interrupted by these followers of Envy, who try vainly to terrify him. Apollo enters followed by the Muses and demigods and heroes.)

APOLLO:

Halt, furious monsters

Flee my features, fear my flames, implacable fury.

ENVY:

No, neither mortals nor the gods, can disarm Envy.

APOLLO:

Do you still dare to follow on my heels?

Do you dare to sustain the dazzle of my light?

ENVY:

I will trouble other regions

That don't see you in your orbit.

APOLLO:

Muses and demigods, avenge me, avenge yourselves.

(The heroes and the demigods seize Envy.)

ENVY:

No, it's in vain that they stop me.

APOLLO:

Choke those serpents that hiss over her head.

ENVY:

They will be reborn a hundred times to serve my wrath.

APOLLO:

Heaven will not allow this monster to perish:

It's immortal like us.

Let him suffer an eternal torture

That by the goodness of the world he may be ill-fated

Let him whine after Glory

Let him be enchained to her throne.

(The cave of Envy is opened and reveals The Temple of Glory. They enchain him to the throne of this goddess.)

CHORUS OF MUSES AND DEMIGODS:

This ever terrible monster

Will always be beaten.

The Arts, Glory, and Virtue

Will nourish his inflexible rage.

APOLLO:

(to The Muses) You, between his horrible cave

And this temple where Glory summons great hearts,

Sing, daughters of the gods, on this peaceable hillock

Glory and the Muses are sisters.

(The cave of Envy ends by vanishing. Two hillocks are seen, cradles decorated with garlands of flowers are halfway up the hill, and the back of the stage is composed of three arcades of greenery through which can be seen the Temple of Glory in the distance.)

APOLLO:

Invest humans with your divine flames

Charm, instruct the universe.

Reign, spread into souls.

The sweetness of your concerts,

Invest humans with your divine flames,

Charm, instruct the universe.

(Dance of Heroes and Muses.)

CHORUS OF MUSES:

We are calming the terrors,

We are singing, we are bringing peace,

But all hearts are not made

To feel the worth of our charms.

A MUSE:

May our laws be forever tractable

In our fields our tender shepherds,

Always simple, always calm

Seek no other honors

Than that, sometimes, far from grandeurs,

Kings shall come into our sanctuaries.

CHORUS OF MUSES:

We are calming the terrors.

We are singing, we are bringing peace,

But all hearts are not made

To feel the worth of our charms.

CURTAIN

ACT II

The stage represents the grove of the Muses. The two sides of the stage are formed by two hills of Parnassus; bowers interlaced with laurels and flowers reign on the inclines of the hills: above them are grottoes pierced by light, decorated with bowers in which are shepherds and shepherdesses. The back is composed of three large bowers.

LIDIA:

Yes, among these shepherds consecrated to the muses

Far from a proud tyrant and flighty lover,

I will find peace, I will calm the storm

Which troubles my frayed emotions.

ARSINE:

In these peaceful retreats

The Muses must calm

Pure hearts, sensitive hearts,

That the court can oppress.

Yet you are weeping; vainly your eye contemplates

These woods, these nymphs, these herdsmen:

Follow the happy example of their tranquility.

LIDIA:

Glory has erected its temple. In these parts,

Shame dwells in our hearts.

Glory, this very day, to the greatest monarch in the world

Must place in his hands an immortal laurel.

Belus is going to obtain it.

ARSINE:

Your profound sorrow

Increases at such a cruel name.

LIDIA:

Belus is going to triumph over enchained Asia

My heart and my estates are in the ranks of the conquered.

The ingrate promised me a brilliant marriage.

He deceived me: at least he won't deceive me anymore.

He is leaving me. I am dying and dying abandoned.

ARSINE:

He betrayed twenty kings; he is betraying your attractions

All he understands is blind power.

LIDIA:

But towards Glory he addresses his steps.

Will he be able to endure my presence without blushing?

ARSINE:

Tyrants don't blush.

LIDIA:

What! So much barbarism with so much valor!

O Muses! Be my support,

Help me against myself.

Don't allow me to love a king who only loves himself.

(The shepherds and shepherdesses consecrated to the Muses emerge from the caves of Parnassus with their rustic instruments.)

LIDIA:

(to shepherds) Come, tender shepherds, you who pity my tears,

Happy mortals inspired by the Muses,

Into my agitated heart pour all the charms

Of Peace that you are celebrating.

CHORUS OF SHEPHERDS:

Do we dare to sing on our weak bagpipes

When horrible trumpets

Have dismayed the echoes?

A SHEPHERDESS:

What do all these heroes want?

Why are they disturbing our retreats?

LIDIA:

They are seeking fortune from the Temple of Glory.

SHEPHERDS:

It's in these parts where you are.

It's in the depth of our heart.

A SHEPHERD:

Towards this Temple where Memory

Consecrates famous names

We no longer raise our eyes.

Shepherds are happy enough

To see, at least, that Glory

Isn't made for them.

(The noise of fifes and trumpets are heard.)

CHORUS OF WARRIORS:

Bloody War,

Death, dismay

Describe our fury.

We make a passage for ourselves

Through carnage

To deeds of grandeur.

SMALL CHORUS OF SHEPHERDS:

What terrifying sounds, what savage uproar!

O Muses! Protect our fortunate regions.

A SHEPHERD:

O Glory, whose name alone has so much attraction

Will this be your language?

(Belus appears under the arbors surrounded by warriors, he is on a throne carried by eight enchained kings.)

BELUS:

Kings, who bear my throne, crowned slaves,

That I have deigned to choose to adorn my victory

Go, go, open for me the Temple of Glory:

Prepare the honors that are destined for me

(he gets down and continues)

I want your pride to second

The cares of my grandeur.

Glory, by elevating me to the first rank in the world

Honors your misfortune sufficiently.

(his suite leaves) (sweet music is heard)

But what tones, filled with softness,

Offend my ear and revolt my heart?

LIDIA:

Great gods, is Humanity a weakness?

Perjured lover, cruel conqueror,

My cries will pursue you without cease.

BELUS:

Your complaints and your cries cannot stop me.

Glory calls me far away from you.

If I were able to listen to you

I would be unworthy of her.

LIDIA:

No, Glory is not barbarous and pitiless.

No, you are making yourself, the gods seem like you.

To their altars you have sacrificed,

Only the tears and blood of miserable mortals.

BELUS:

Don't condemn my exploits.

When one intends to make oneself master,

One is, sometimes, despite oneself,

More cruel than one wishes to be.

LIDIA:

How I hate your lucky exploits.

How fate has changed you, how grandeur has distracted you.

Perhaps you were born generous;

Your good fortune has rendered you barbarous.

BELUS:

I was born to master, to change the universe.

The weak bird in a grove

Makes its sweet concerts heard.

The eagle which flies on high

Brings thunderbolts and devastation.

Stop trying to stop me with your useless murmurs

And let me fulfill my august destiny.

(Belus leaves to go into the temple.)

LIDIA:

O Muses, powerful goddesses!

Bend the pride of this ambitious man,

Aid me against his cruelty,

Or at least against my weaknesses.

(Apollo and his Muses descend in a chariot which rests its two ends on the two hills of Parnassus.)

APOLLO AND THE MUSES:

(singing in chorus) We will soften

With our likeable arts

Pitiless hearts;

Or we will punish them.

APOLLO:

Shepherds, who in these groves

Learned our divine songs,

You calm savage monsters,

Bend cruel humans.

(The shepherds dance,)

APOLLO:

Fly, Love, god of gods, embellish my empire,

Disarm war in its fury,

With a look, with a smile, with a word,

You calm disorder and horror,

You can change a heart;

I can only instruct it.

Fly, Love, god of gods, embellish my empire

Disarm war in its fury.

BELUS:

(returning followed by warriors)

What! This temple doesn't yet open for me!

What! This glory that I adore,

Nearby these parts prepared my altars,

And I only see weak mortals

And weak gods I never knew of.

CHORUS OF SHEPHERDS:

You've made yourself feared enough.

Now make yourself cherished.

Ah! how a great heart is to be pitied

When nothing can soften it.

A SHEPHERDESS:

You betrayed the attractions

Of a tender and submissive beauty.

Cruel conqueror, don't hope

That Glory will favor you.

A SHEPHERD:

What! He directs his steps toward Glory

And his heart is unfaithful?

Ah! Among us the torture of ingrates

Is an eternal shame.

BELUS:

What do I hear? There's a crowd of people who offend me!

Whose is the weak voice that murmurs in these parts

When earth trembles in silence?

Soldiers, deliver me from these odious people.

CHORUS OF MUSES:

Stop! Respect the gods

Who protect innocence.

BELUS:

Gods! Do they dare suspend my vengeance?

APOLLO AND THE MUSES:

Heaven, cover yourself with fire, thunders burst,

Tremble, flee the irritated gods.

(Thunder and lightning emerge from the Chariot of Apollo and the Muses.)

APOLLO:

Far from the Temple of Glory

Run to the Temple of Fury.

There they will guard your eternal memory

With an eternal horror.

CHORUS OF APOLLO AND THE MUSES.

Implacable heart

Learn to tremble.

Death pursues you, death must immolate you.

This guilty fortunate

Implacable heart

Learn to tremble.

BELUS:

I never tremble; I brave thunder.

I scorn this temple, and I hate humans

With my powerful hands I will set ablaze

The sad remains of earth.

CHORUS:

Implacable heart

Learn to tremble.

Death pursues you, death must immolate

This guilty fortunate.

Implacable heart

Learn to tremble.

APOLLO AND THE MUSES:

(to Lidia)

You who tremble for a deplorable lover

Extinguish your fires, break his bonds.

Taste through our blessings

An unalterable calm.

(The shepherds and shepherdesses lead Lidia away.)

CURTAIN

ACT III

The stage represents the avenue leading to the front of the Temple of Glory. The throne prepared for the one who must be named the greatest of mankind is seen at the back of the stage. It is supported by Virtues, and is reached by several steps.

The High Priest of Glory, crowned with laurels, a palm in hand, surrounded by priests and priestesses of Glory.

A PRIESTESS:

Glory, the enchantress,

Superb mistress

Of kings and conquerors,

Of ardent youth

And frosty age,

They seek your favors.

CHORUS:

Glory, the enchantress, etc.

PRIESTESS:

The pretended philosopher

Believes he's broken free

Of your noble slavery.

He's abused.

He's a scorned lover.

His scorn is homage.

THE HIGH PRIEST:

Goddess of heroes, of true philosophers, and of kings

Noble and fruitful source

Of virtues and of exploits,

O noble Glory! It's here that your powerful voice

Must designate by an exact choice

The first of masters of the world.

Come, fly, run,

Arbitress of peace, and thunderbolt of war,

You who subdue, you who calm the earth,

We are going to crown the worthiest of you.

(Dance of heroes with priestesses of Glory.)

(The followers of Bacchus arrive with some bacchantes and maenads crowned with ivy, thyrsus in hand.)

A WARRIOR (following Bacchus)

Bacchus is in all places our invincible guide.

This proud and beneficent hero

Is always friendly and terrible.

Prepare the prize which awaits him.

A BACCHANTE AND THE CHORUS:

The god of pleasures is going to appear.

We are announcing our master;

His sweet furies devour our hearts.

(During this chorus the priests of Glory reenter the temple, whose doors are then shut.)

THE WARRIOR:

Enchained tigers are escorting to earth

Bacchus and Erigone:

The victorious, the vanquished,

All the gods of pleasures, all the gods of war

Are marching together confounded.

(Bacchus and Erigone appear together on a chariot drawn by tigers, surrounded by warriors, bacchantes, Egyptians, and satyrs.)

BACCHUS:

Erigone, object full of charms,

Object of my burning ardor,

I didn't invent, in the horror of struggles,

This nectar of humans, necessary to happiness,

To console the earth and wipe away tears.

Rather, it was to enflame your heart.

Let's banish reason from our brilliant celebrations.

No, I never know it

In my pleasures, in my conquests

No, I adore you, and I hate it.

Let's banish reason from our brilliant celebrations.

ERIGONE:

Rather conserve it to augment your flames,

Banish only uproar and havoc.

If through you the world is happy,

I will love you more.

BACCHUS:

Weak feelings offend my love,

I want only eternal intoxication.

Glory, grandeur, pleasure, tenderness,

Reign over my senses in turn.

ERIGONE:

You alarm my heart; it trembles with surrender.

By your passions it is dismayed,

It would be more distracted,

If yours was more tender.

BACCHUS:

Share my divine transports

On my victorious chariot, in the breast of tenderness

Make heaven jealous: enchain humanity.

A god more powerful than I drags us and hurries us.

Let the thyrsus reign forever

In pleasures and in war

Let it reign instead of thunder

And with arrows of love.

CHORUS:

Let the thyrsus reign forever

In pleasures and in war.

Let it reign instead of thunder

And with arrows of love.

ERIGONE:

What god seizes my soul!

What impetuous disorder!

He troubles my heart, he distracts it.

Love alone makes for greater happiness.

BACCHUS:

But what is this solitary temple doing in these parts.

To what gods is it consecrated?

I am conqueror, I knew how to please you.

If Bacchus is known, Bacchus is adored.

ONE OF THE FOLLOWERS OF BACCHUS:

In these parts Glory is the only God they adore.

Today she must place on her altars

The most august of mortals,

The beneficent conqueror of nations, at dawn

Shall have these solemn honors.

ERIGONE:

Such a brilliant homage

Cannot be refused;

Love alone guided me to this happy shore.

But one can divert one's steps

When Glory is in the way.

TOGETHER:

Glory is a vain error,

But with you it's supreme happiness.

It's you that I love.

It's you that fill my heart.

BACCHUS:

The Temple's opening.

Glory's revealing herself.

The object of my ardor will be crowned.

Follow me.

(The Temple of Glory seems open.)

HIGH PRIEST OF GLORY:

Bold one, stop.

This laurel will be profaned

If it crowns your head.

Bacchus, that they celebrate in these parts,

Finds no preference here.

There is a vast distance

Between name recognition and names that are glorious.

ERIGONE:

Eh, what! With her gifts is Glory avaricious

For his more brilliant favors?

BACCHUS:

I've poured blessings on a submissive universe.

For whom are these laurels that your hand is preparing?

THE HIGH PRIEST:

For virtues of the highest price.

Bacchus, content yourself with reigning in your celebrations

And drowning all the ills that your furors have caused.

Let us crown more beautiful conquests

And greater blessings.

BACCHUS:

Vain people, proud people, children of sorrow

You don't deserve gifts so precious

Bacchus abandons you to frigid wisdom

He knows no better way to punish you.

Fly, follow me, lovable troupe,

Come embellish other parts.

With the hand of pleasures, Cupids and games,

Pour this delectable nectar,

Conqueror of mortals and of gods.

Fly, follow me, lovable troupe,

Come embellish other parts.

BACCHUS AND ERIGONE:

Let's course the earth

At the whim of our desires.

From the temple of Glory

To the Temple of Pleasures.

(They dance.)

A BACCHANTE:

(with the chorus)

Bacchus, soft and proud conqueror,

Lead my steps, reign in my heart.

Glory promises happiness,

Yet it's Bacchus who gives it to us.

Reason, you are only an error

And pain surrounds you.

Pleasure, you are not a deceiver,

My soul abandons itself to you.

Bacchus, soft and proud conqueror, etc.

CURTAIN

ACT IV

The stage represents the villa of Atraxate, half ruined in the midst of which is a public square decorated with a triumphal arch, hung with trophies.

PLAUTINA:

Come back, divine Trajan, sweet and terrible conqueror.

The world is my rival; all hearts are yours.

But is there a heart more tender

That adores you more than I?

The Parthians have fallen beneath your thundering hand;

You punish, you avenge kings.

Rome is happy and triumphant

Your good deeds surpass your exploits.

Come back, divine Trajan, sweet and terrible conqueror.

The world is my rival, all hearts are yours.

But is there a heart more tender

That adores you more than I?

FANIA:

In this barbarous region, in the breast of Armenia

Do you dare confront the horrors of combat?

PLAUTINA:

We were protected by his powerful genius.

And love guided my steps.

JUNIA:

Europe will again see its avenger and master;

They say he's going to appear under these triumphal arches.

PLAUTINA:

They were erected by my hands,

What sweet pleasure succeeds my profound sorrow.

In the master of the world we are going to behold

The most lovable of humans.

JUNIA:

Our triumphant soldiers, enriched, full of glory,

Are flying his name to the heavens.

FANIA:

He's stealing their songs of victory;

Alone, without pomp, or followers,

He's coming to ornament these parts.

PLAUTINA:

Pomp and the dazzle of honors

Are necessary to vulgar heroes.

For vain grandeurs

These supports are necessary.

Trajan alone is followed by his immortal glory.

One imagines one is seeing the universe near him at its knees.

And it's for me he's coming! This hero is faithful to me!

Great Gods. You dwell in his beautiful soul

And I share it with you.

(Trajan enters and Plautina runs to greet him.)

PLAUTINA:

At last I see you again,

The charm of my life

Is returned to me forever.

TRAJAN:

Heaven sells me these blessings dearly.

I return one moment to tear myself from you,

To animate myself with a new virtue,

To deserve, when Mars calls me,

To be Emperor of Rome and to be your spouse.

PLAUTINA:

What are you saying? What a funereal word!

One moment, you, o heaven! A single moment remains to me.

When my life depends on always seeing you again.

TRAJAN:

Heaven has at all times granted me its aid.

Soon it will return me to the charms I adore.

It's for you my heart was made.

I have seen you, and I will be conqueror.

PLAUTINA:

What! Aren't you already a conqueror?

What! Is there yet

A king your hand has not disarmed?

From dawn to sunset hasn't everything submitted to you?

Isn't the universe calm?

TRAJAN:

They are daring to betray me.

PLAUTINA:

No, I cannot believe you.

They can't make you break your word.

TRAJAN:

With defeated Parthians the inexorable king,

Irritated by his fall, braves my victory.

Five kings that he seduced are armed against me.

They've joined trickery to excess of rage,

They are at the foot of these ramparts.

But on my side, I have the gods, the Romans,

My courage and my love and your glances.

PLAUTINA:

My glances will follow you,

I intend that on my head

Heaven wear out its wrath.

I won't leave you; I will brave their blows,

I will decoy the death they are readying for you.

At least, I will die near you.

TRAJAN:

Ah! Don't overwhelm me to this degree,

My heart is too sensitive.

Ah! Allow me to deserve you.

You love me, it suffices: nothing is impossible to me.

Nothing can resist me.

PLAUTINA:

Cruel, can you stop me?

Already, I hear the shouts of the perfidious enemy.

TRAJAN:

I hear the voice of duty which guides me.

I fly: stay here: victory is following me.

I fly: await all of my intrepid people

And love which leads me.

TOGETHER:

I am going to punish a barbarian.

Go punish a barbarian,

Grind them under my feet,

Grind them under your feet,

The enemy that separates us,

That snatches me for a moment from you.

PLAUTINA:

He abandons me to my mortal sorrow.

Dear lover, stop. Ah! Turn your eyes,

See mine once again.

TRAJAN:

(at the back of the stage)

O Gods, o just gods

Watch over the empire and over her!

PLAUTINA:

He's already far from these parts.

Duty, are you satisfied? I am dying and I admire him.

Ministers of the god of war,

Priestesses of Venus who watch over the empire,

Pierce heaven with shouts, accompany my steps,

Second the love which inspires me.

CHORUS OF PRIESTS OF MARS:

Proud god of alarms,

Protect our arms,

Lead our standards.

CHORUS OF PRIESTESS OF VENUS:

Goddess of graces,

Fly on our tracks,

Enchain the god Mars.

(They Dance.)

CHORUS OF PRIESTESSES:

Mother of Rome and peaceful loves,

Come arrange everything under your charming law.

Come crown our invincible Romans.

They are all born for love and for you.

PLAUTINA:

Powerful gods, protect your living image!

Once you were mortals like him.

It's for having reigned as he reigns today

That heaven is your share.

(They dance.)

(A chorus of Romans can be heard advancing slowly onto the stage.)

Charming heroes, who could believe

In exploits so prompt and so great?

In the least of time you make

The most enduring memory.

JUNIA:

Do you hear those shouts and those songs of victory?

FANIA:

Trajan is returning conqueror.

PLAUTINA:

Could you have doubted it?

I see these captive kings, ornaments of his glory.

He's just fought them; he's just subdued them.

JUNIA:

Before punishing them under his legitimate laws,

Before striking his victims,

At your knees he wants to present them.

(Trajan appears surrounded by Roman eagles and fasces; the conquered kings are in his train.)

TRAJAN:

Kings, who dread my vengeance,

Who fear the affronts destined for the vanquished,

Be henceforth enchained

Solely by gratitude.

Plautina is hereabouts, in her presence

There must be no unfortunates.

THE KINGS:

(rising, singing with the chorus)

O grandeur! O clemency!

Conqueror equal to the gods,

You have their power,

Like them, you pardon.

PLAUTINA:

Your virtues surpass even my hope;

My heart is more touched than those of these kings.

TRAJAN:

Ah! If there are virtues in this heart that loves you,

You know to whom I owe them.

I wanted humans to deserve the suffrage,

To subdue kings, to break their fetters,

And to bring you my homage

With the vows of the universe.

Heavens! What do I see around here?

(Glory descends in headlong flight, a crown of laurel in hand.)

GLORY:

You see your reward.

The prize of your exploits, especially your clemency.

My throne is at your feet; you reign with me.

(The scene changes and represents the Temple of Glory.)

GLORY:

(continuing) More than one hero,

More than one great king,

Vainly jealous of his memory,

Flew always towards Glory

And Glory flies after you.

(The followers of Glory mix with the Romans and form dances.)

A ROMAN:

Reign in peace after so many storms,

Triumph in our contented hearts.

Fate presides over battles, over devastation,

Glory is in the blessings.

Thunder, spare our happy shores,

Peaceful calm, return forever,

Reign in peace, etc.

CHORUS:

Heaven seconds us,

Let's celebrate its choice,

Examples for kings,

Delight of the world,

Let's live under your laws.

JUNIA:

Tender Venus, to whom Rome has submitted,

To our exploits join your tender attractions,

Order Mars, enchanted in your arms

That for Trajan his favor be perpetuated.

CHORUS:

Heaven seconds us,

Let's celebrate its choice,

Example for kings,

Delight of the world,

Let's live under your laws.

TRAJAN:

Honors so brilliant are too much for my share.

Gods, whose favor I experience,

Gods of my people, complete your work,

Change this august temple into one of happiness;

Let it serve forever to celebrate

Fortunate humans;

Let it last as long as the conquests

And the glory of Romans.

GLORY:

The Gods refuse nothing

To heroes who resemble them.

Fly Pleasures that his virtue resembles

The Temple of happiness will always be mine.

CURTAIN

ACT V

The stage represents the Temple of Happiness; it is formed with a pavilion by a light construction, with peristyles, gardens, fountains, etc.; this delightful place is filled by Romans of all conditions.

CHORUS:

Let's sing on this solemn day

And may the earth reply to us.

A mortal, a single mortal

Has made the world's happiness.

(They dance.)

A ROMAN GIRL:

All ranks, all sexes, all ages

Must aspire to happiness.

CHORUS:

All ranks, all sexes, all ages

Must aspire to happiness.

THE ROMAN GIRL:

Capricious Spring,

Summer full of passion,

Autumn wiser,

Reason, banter

Isolation, grandeur

All ranks, all sexes, all ages

Must aspire to happiness.

CHORUS:

All ranks, all sexes, all ages

Must aspire to happiness.

(Some shepherds and shepherdesses enter and dance.)

A SHEPHERDESS:

Here the most brilliant flowers

Do not efface the violets.

Standards and shepherds crooks

Are decorated with the same colors.

The songs of our tender shepherds

Mingle with the uproar of trumpets.

Love revives in these retreats

All glances and all hearts.

Here the most brilliant flowers

Do not efface the violets.

Standards and shepherds crooks

Are decorated with the same colors.

(Romans join in dancing with the shepherds and shepherdesses.)

A ROMAN:

On a day so fine

There are no alarms,

Mars is without arms,

Cupid without blindfold.

CHORUS:

On a day so fine

There are no alarms,

Mars is without arms,

Cupid without blindfold.

ROMAN:

Glory and Cupid hereabouts have no wings

Except to fly into our arms.

Glory to her enemies presents our soldiers,

And Cupid presents them our beauties.

CHORUS:

On a day so fine

There are no alarms,

Mars is without arms,

Cupid without blindfold.

(They dance.)

(Trajan appears with Plautina, and all the Romans form up around him.)

CHORUS:

You that Victory

Crowns on this day,

Your most beautiful glory

Comes from tender Cupid.

TRAJAN:

O nation of heroes who love me, and that I love,

You make my splendor.

I intend to reign in your hearts

(pointing to Plautina)

On so much attraction, and on myself,

Rise to high heaven, incense that I receive

Return towards the gods, homage that I attract.

Gods, always protect this formidable empire

Always inspire all its kings.

Rise to high heaven, incense that I receive

Return to the gods, homage that I attract.

(All the different troupes resume their dancing around Trajan and Plautina and end the celebration in a general ballet.)

CURTAIN

ACT II VARIANT

LIDIA:

Muses, daughters of heaven,

Peace reigns in your celebrations,

You suspend mortals' sorrows;

In the hearts of humans you calm storms,

Serene days are born from your favors.

Love, leave my heart; love break my chain

Belus is abandoning me today;

Vengeful scorn, too just hate

Be, if possible, my support.

Love, leave my heart; Love break my chain,

Don't be a tyrant like him.

ARSINE:

The Muses sometimes calm a sensitive heart.

And to implore them you are leaving your court.

But fear being sought out by this invincible warrior.

To the Temple of Glory he flies in broad day

He will be more inflexible.

LIDIA:

No, I want in his heart to carry repentance.

Here he's seeking glory; and that name reassures me.

Glory cannot choose

An unjust and perjured conqueror.

Alas! I thought him virtuous.

How fate has changed him! How his grandeur distracts him!

I thought him beneficent, sensitive, generous!

His good fortune has rendered him barbaric.

ARSINE:

He insults the kings that have succumbed to his valor,

Vengeance marches before him.

Pride, Pomp, Terror,

And Love flees from his presence.

LIDIA:

What crimes, O heaven! With how much valor!

Goddesses of these parts, support innocence.

Console my alarmed heart,

Help me against myself.

And don't allow me to love

A hero intoxicated with his supreme splendor,

Who is no longer worthy of being loved.

(The shepherds and shepherdesses enter and dance to the sound of bagpipes.)

LIDIA:

Come, tender shepherds, you who pity my tears,

Happy mortals, by muses inspired,

In my agitated heart spread the charms

Of the peace that you celebrate

CHORUS OF SHEPHERDS:

Dare we sing with our weak bagpipes,

When horrible trumpets have terrified the echoes?

A SHEPHERDESS:

We are fleeing before this hero

Who is coming to trouble our retreats.

LIDIA:

Don't flee Belus; employ the art of gods

To make this proud heart bow before virtue.

The Muses in their groves

Inspire your divine songs;

You calm savage monsters,

Enchant cruel humans.

CHORUS:

Let's enchant cruel humans.

(They resume their dances.)

A SHEPHERDESS:

The god of fine arts can alone instruct us

But only Love can change hearts

To soften them he must seduce them

Only the features of the god of Love are conquerors.

(They dance.)

A SHEPHERDESS:

Descend, charming god, come show your harp,

Come form the sound of the god of the nine sisters,

Lend to virtue your voice, your smile,

Your features, your torch, your chains of flowers.

(They dance.)

A SHEPHERD:

Towards this temple where Memory

Consecrates famous names,

We are not raising our eyes.

The shepherds are happy enough

To see at least Glory

Isn't made for them.

(A noise of trumpets and kettle drums is heard.)

CHORUS OF WARRIORS:

(entering) Bloody war

Death, terror,

Signal our furors

Making a passage for us

Through carnage

To acts of grandeur.

CHORUS OF SHEPHERDS:

What horrifying sounds, what savage uproar!

O Muses, shelter our fortunate regions!

A SHEPHERD:

O Glory, whose name seems to have so much appeal.

Will this be your language?

CHORUS OF WARRIORS:

Lightning embraces the heavens,

Thunder threatens the earth.

Do you declare, great gods,

With your thunderous voice

That Belus is arriving in these parts?

(enter Belus.)

BELUS:

Where am I? What have I seen?

No, I cannot believe it.

This temple which is owed me,

This haven of Glory,

Is closed to me?

My soldiers have gone pale with fright,

Thunder has devoured the bloody spoils

That I was going to consecrate to Mars.

My standards are broken

In my triumphant hands.

Implacable gods, jealous gods,

What have I done that outrages you?

I've made the universe tremble under my blows,

I've put kings at my feet,

And their subjects in slavery,

I am avenged like you,

What more are you asking?

CHORUS OF SHEPHERDS:

One doesn't imitate the gods

By means of the horrors of war.

To be loved by them

One must make oneself loved on earth.

A SHEPHERDESS:

A king that nothing will soften,

Is of kings, the most to be pitied.

Soon he'll make himself shiver

When he keeps frightening others.

CHORUS OF SHEPHERDS:

A king that nothing will soften,

Is of kings, the most to be pitied.

Soon he'll make himself shiver

When he keeps frightening others.

BELUS:

What! In these parts they brave my fury

When at my feet the world is silent in terror?

(the sound of bagpipes is heard)

An unknown pleasure surprises and enchants me,

Even in the breast of horror.

(the bagpipes continue)

From the innocent candor of these simple shepherds

Its sweetness makes itself felt in my astonished heart.

A SHEPHERDESS:

A king, if he wants to be happy

Must fulfill our vows;

True happiness crowns him

When he gives it.

In palaces, in forests,

They cherish his sweet laws.

He tastes, he pours in all parts

The beneficence of the gods.

At his voice virtues are reborn.

Smiles, games caress him,

Glory and Love

Share his court.

In his supreme blood,

It's he alone that is loved.

It's he more than his favors

That charms hearts.

A king if he wants to be happy,

Is of kings, the most to be pitied.

Soon he'll make himself shiver

When he keeps frightening others.

CHORUS OF SHEPHERDS:

A king whom nothing softens

Is of kings the most to be pitied

Soon he'll make himself shiver

As he makes himself feared.

THE SHEPHERDESS:

Listen to the god in our fields who inspires us.

Make all hearts satisfied,

Soften the empire of your strict laws,

Glory is in beneficence.

CHORUS:

A king that nothing can soften,

Is of kings, the most to be pitied.

Soon he'll make himself shiver

When he keeps frightening others.

BELUS:

The more I listen to their songs,

The more sensitive I am becoming.

Gods! Have you led me into this peaceable domain

To enlighten a new day for me?

Flatterers were blinding me; they were leading their master astray.

And shepherds are making me know

What I was unaware of in my court.

LIDIA:

Learn even more: see all my flame.

I followed you into these parts.

For you I asked the gods

To soften, to touch your soul.

Your virtues once knew how to enflame me

You left everything for the horror of war.

Ah! I would like to see you adored on earth

Even though you loved me no more.

BELUS:

That's too much, I give in to the charm which attracts me.

Perhaps I would have braved the empire of the gods.

But they borrow your voice,

They have guided your steps, their bounty inspires you;

I am disarmed, I sigh.

I dare hope that one day I will obtain, under your laws,

The immortal glory to which I aspire.

These gods, grantors of my vows,

Will appease their wrath

And by deserving to please you

I will render mortals happy.

LIDIA AND BELUS:

Descend from the heavens, hurl your flames,

Triumph, Love, god of great hearts,

Animate virtues and noble ardors

Which must reign in our souls.

CHORUS:

Between Glory and Cupids,

In a profound peace,

Go you both to the world to give

Just laws and beautiful days.

CURTAIN

ABOUT THE TRANSLATOR

Frank J. Morlock has written and translated many plays since retiring from the legal profession in 1992. His translations have also appeared on Project Gutenberg, the Alexandre Dumas Père web page, Literature in the Age of Napoléon, Infinite Artistries.com, and Munsey's (formerly Blackmask). In 2006 he received an award from the North American Jules Verne Society for his translations of Verne's plays. He lives and works in México.

www.ingramcontent.com/pod-product-compliance
Lightning Source LLC
LaVergne TN
LVHW041618070426
835507LV00008B/311